SHINE THROUGH THE STORM

RESILIENCE, WELLNESS, AND THE POWER OF SHOWING UP EVERY DAY

TAMMY DOTSON

Limits of Liability / Disclaimer of Warranty

The authors and publisher of this book and the accompanying materials have used their best efforts in preparing this program. The authors and publisher make no representation or warranties with respect to the accuracy, applicability, fitness, or completeness of the contents of this program. They disclaim any warranties (expressed or implied), merchantability, or fitness for any particular purpose. The authors and publisher shall in no event be held liable for any loss or other damages, including but not limited to special, incidental, consequential, or other damages. As always, the advice of a competent legal, tax, accounting or other professional should be sought. The authors and publisher do not warrant the performance, effectiveness or applicability of any sites listed in this book. All links are for information purposes only and are not warranted for content, accuracy or any other implied or explicit purpose.

Time2shineconsulting.com

Riverview, FL 33579

DEDICATION

This book is dedicated to my daughters Taja and Victoria! I would also like to thank all the people that played a part in this project. It was definitely a marathon and not a sprint but you believed in me, even when I didn't believe in myself. You pushed me, you held me accountable, you challenged me, and you celebrated with me.

THANK YOU!

In Loving Memory

Of

Geraldine I. Dotson

TABLE OF CONTENTS

EMBRACE YOUR JOURNEY: INTRODUCING "SHINE THROUGH THE STORM"

Hello, beautiful souls! I'm Tammy Dotson, and I am overjoyed that you have chosen to be part of this remarkable journey by picking up SHINE Through the Storm. You may be wondering what lies within these pages, and I'm here to give you a glimpse of the empowerment waiting to unfold as you delve into your reading.

Life can often feel like a raging storm, with obstacles and challenges that threaten to drown out our inner light. As women, we juggle so many responsibilities, wear numerous hats, and face personal battles that can leave us feeling lost and overwhelmed. I want to tell you that you are not alone. You have the strength and resilience to navigate through these storms, and this book is a compass designed to guide you back to your true self.

In SHINE Through the Storm, I share not only my life experiences but also the hard-earned lessons I've learned along the way. I've faced my share of challenges—from living with Alopecia since I was 23 to overcoming diagnosis with Sjögren's Disease in my late 40s, followed by major brain surgery in 2020 to remove a cavernoma. These hurdles have shaped me in profound ways, teaching me that resilience is not just a buzzword; it is a vital skill that each of us can cultivate.

Through rigorous training for 17 marathons to include six world major marathons, 92 half marathons, and even completing an IRONMAN®, I learned that true strength comes from perseverance and determination. It's not always about the finish line; sometimes, it's about the journey and how we rise when challenges try to knock us down. I want you to visualize yourself crossing finish lines in your own life, reclaiming your strength, and rediscovering your purpose.

As you read through this book, you will find practical tools and encouragement to help you weather life's storms with clarity and focus. My greatest hope is that you will feel empowered to prevent the mistakes I made and that my journey can serve as a beacon for yours. Each page has been crafted with love and care, so you can learn to navigate obstacles with newfound lightness and determination.

Hold this book close; it is not just a collection of words; it is a testament to the power that lies within you. So, let's do this together! Turn the page, begin the adventure, and embrace the brilliance that awaits on the other side of your storm. You have already taken the most courageous step by investing in yourself, and I can't wait to walk this path with you.

Remember, it's never too late to reclaim who you are and shine bright, even in the darkest of times. Here's to your journey of resilience and self-discovery!

Happy reading,

CHAPTER 1

THE DIAGNOSIS THAT DIDN'T DEFINE ME

Receiving a diagnosis can be one of the most challenging moments in a person's life.

Facing the Storm

For me, it felt like an unexpected storm had rolled in, darkening the skies and threatening my sense of self. When I learned that I had Sjögren's (SHOW-GRINS) disease and alopecia, I was flooded with emotions—fear, confusion, and sadness. This chapter is not just about the moment I heard the news; it's about the journey that followed and how I refused to let those diagnoses become the limits of who I am.

A Life-Changing Morning

At 23 years old, I woke up to a sight that would change my life forever: clumps of my hair scattered across my pillow. My scalp felt like it was on fire, a painful reminder of the chemical relaxers that had become a routine part of my beauty regimen. I had thought it was a mishap at the hair salon—perhaps my beautician left the relaxer in too long or didn't wash it out properly. I was flooded with thoughts, various scenarios spinning through my mind like a whirling dervish.

In desperate need of relief, I rushed to the Emergency Room. My mind was racing with concerns, but the doctor's dismissive diagnosis of an "allergic reaction" left me unsatisfied. I received some ointment for the sores and a prescription for Benadryl, but my hair continued to thin, and my worries persisted.

The Struggle and the Search

I didn't learn my lesson; I kept relying on relaxers, convinced that I could salvage my hair if I simply asked for a milder solution or a shorter application time. Each unsuccessful attempt left me with more sores and less hair, yet I held on, hoping against hope that maybe, just maybe, it would work out.

It wasn't until 2001, while living in South Korea, that everything changed.

A New Diagnosis, A New Challenge

I visited a doctor for other concerns and he casually mentioned the bald spots I had been hiding beneath my long hair. That one large, circular bald spot in the middle of my head had become a constant source of anxiety. The doctor's words struck me hard: "I believe you have alopecia. And not just alopecia, but Central Centrifugal Cicatricial Alopecia (CCCA)." The term felt foreign and heavy, but hearing it was a relief—I finally had a name for my struggle.

For the next 20 years, I wrestled with my self-image and how I interacted with the world.

The Weight of Change

The hidden bald spot became a significant part of my life, and though I masked it with hairdos and hairsprays, the feeling of not being in control gnawed at me. I tried every hair regrowth option available, only to find that they all fell short of expectations. The focus became less about regrowing what I lost and more about preventing the spread of my condition.

But the journey didn't end there. In 2020, I faced another storm—this time in the form of Sjögren's disease.

Entering Another Battle

The years leading up to the diagnosis were filled with chronic pain and fatigue, the kind that drained the joy from day-to-day living. My doctors couldn't pinpoint what was wrong. Was it stress? An early sign of menopause? It felt like a never-ending cycle of doctors and specialists, none of whom could provide clarity. I endured years on a daily nonsteroidal anti-inflammatory drug, only to be told that a brain bleed necessitated stopping the medication cold turkey. That change threw my body into chaos.

My symptoms fluctuated daily—one day my eyes burned, the next my joints ached, and the relentless fatigue turned even the simplest tasks into monumental challenges. It was during a visit to my podiatrist that I first felt a glimmer of hope. He identified that something autoimmune was at play and urged me to consult a rheumatologist. Several tests later, and the source of the mystery revealed itself: Sjögren's disease.

I remember the weight of that diagnosis.

Acceptance and Awareness

It came on a Thursday just before Labor Day weekend, delivered through a notification stating my lab results were ready to be viewed. This was at the height of the COVID-19 pandemic when visits were through telehealth. I logged on, eager to learn what the lab results held. The moment I saw "positive for Sjögren's," tears of relief streamed down my face. Of course, my first instinct was "what in the world is this funny-looking word," But finally, I had an answer. After feeling dismissed and misunderstood for so long, it was a turning point, yet at the same time, it unknotted a web of worries for my future.

At first, hearing that I had Sjögren's disease—a condition that affects moisture-producing glands, leading to symptoms like dry mouth and fatigue—was overwhelming. The woman who sprinted through life, tackling challenges one after another, suddenly felt trapped in a body that seemed to betray her. On the outside, I always presented strong and capable, the type who loved to take on everything from physical training to professional pursuits. Yet within me, a storm brewed. I struggled with self-doubt and internal critique, whispering that perhaps I was weak, that I couldn't face these new realities. But soon, through a journey laced with painful realizations and unexpected sources of support, I learned that my diagnosis would not define me.

After getting the results, I immediately reached out to a dear friend, sharing my news. "I finally have answers!" I told her, feeling a huge weight lift off my shoulders. "It's such a relief!" The positivity in her voice matched my own as she celebrated with me.

I spent hours on the internet that day, trying to learn everything I could about Sjögren's disease. I wanted to understand it so that I could share my knowledge with others, to advocate for myself and those who might face a similar situation. The more I read, the more empowered I felt, but honestly, the journey was still daunting.

The initial perception of myself shattered like glass, revealing doubts and insecurities that I hadn't acknowledged before.

Finding My Voice

I remember looking in the mirror, noticing the hair falling away, and being struck by a crushing sadness. I had always identified myself by my energy, my ability to go and go, and my passion for life. Now, with a diagnosis like alopecia, I felt stripped of part of my identity. Add to that the fatigue and discomfort of Sjögren's disease, and I felt as though half of me had faded away.

I felt embarrassed and defeated, unhappy with how my body was changing. Friends and family stared at me, perhaps unable to fathom what I was experiencing. People often struggle to understand illnesses that are invisible, especially chronic issues like Sjögren's—where the struggle is not always apparent to onlookers.

As I shared the news at work, I was navigating a path of uncertainty, wondering if my condition would allow me to continue my military career. That added another layer of anxiety to my situation. At work, my challenges presented a different set of obstacles. As a member of the military, I had always prided myself on my ability to power through fatigue. But as my symptoms worsened, I found myself dozing off in meetings or retreating to my car for quick naps just to regain energy for the day. I felt embarrassed to admit that no matter how much sleep I got, I still struggled with fatigue. Friends and colleagues made light-hearted comments, suggesting I needed to get more sleep or asking if I partied too late the night before. Each joke stung, reminding me that they did not understand what I was going through.

I quickly realized that the fear of judgment loomed larger than the illness itself. Unfounded worries plagued my mind: What if my colleagues thought I was lazy? What if they believed I wasn't capable of performing my duties? This anxiety began to build resentment toward my illness. I felt isolated, especially since I lacked the support from my supervisors at work. They didn't fully grasp the implications of my struggles—or maybe they didn't want to. It didn't help that I was out of the office a majority of the time attending specialist appointments. I often fought against the anxiety that stemmed from feeling misunderstood, wanting to prove myself even more when all I needed was a bit of empathy.

Since I didn't have anyone nearby to rely on for support, I leaned heavily on my run buddy and friends who were far away. These bonds became vital lifelines. They encouraged me to be my own advocate, to not stop seeking the answers I needed. This pushed me to seek out support groups online, talk to other patients, and immerse myself in the advocacy world.

I learned that I was not alone, that many others faced similar challenges and that people could be affected by this "invisible disease" in various ways.

Empowerment Through Action

One of the most uplifting moments was when I shared my experience online. Soon, my story caught the attention of the incoming CEO of the Sjogren's Foundation, who reached out to ask if I would be interested in joining their board of directors. I didn't hesitate. This opportunity felt like a chance to make a real impact. Watching Janet—an influential leader battling the same disease—navigating life with sheer grace fueled my desire to rise above my diagnosis. I absorbed the wisdom that it's not about accepting the limitations placed on us but finding ways to redefine what's possible under the new circumstances. I was determined to create a new normal and achieve as much quality of life as I could.

Joining the Sjögren's Foundation board of directors changed my relationship with the diagnosis.

Shifting Perspectives

My voice was now included in discussions with medical professionals, and I had the chance to advocate for patient rights and awareness. I remember attending a national patient conference and sharing my experiences. People approached me afterward, thanking me for the information and support. They wanted to know how they could find a healthcare team that would listen to them and take their pain seriously. Hearing personal stories from other patients showed me how important advocacy is in creating a real change in the healthcare system.

I learned quickly that both Sjögren's and alopecia are autoimmune disorders, but they affect life in very different ways. Alopecia was more cosmetic, a struggle tied up in physical appearance. As a woman, my hair felt like a crown; losing it was deeply tied to my self-worth. I remember feeling paranoid in social situations, always worried that people were staring at my bald spots. There were moments when I would catch a stranger's gaze, feeling their judgment consume me.

In stark contrast, Sjögren's was more about how I functioned daily. It affected my ability to do things I once took for granted. Fatigue and brain fog began to dictate my life. I often worried that my forgetfulness would make me seem flaky or unorganized, and it chest-pounded with frustration every time I struggled to communicate. As someone who used to pride myself on being articulate and perfectly organized, it was a constant battle to accept that I was no longer that version of myself.

Yet through it all, there were people who played a pivotal role in reshaping my self-worth. I think back to the Army doctor who first diagnosed my alopecia. He understood the complexities of ethnic hairstyling and helped me realize that my struggles were valid. His confirmation shifted my perception of self, and I felt empowered to take control of my hair health. The journey continued under the guidance of another doctor, Dr. Akbari, who promoted a natural approach to scalp health. With her, I learned to cut back on harmful chemicals and focus on nurturing my growing hair.

And then there was India Arie's song, "I Am Not My Hair." That anthem offered liberation. It emboldened me to take risks with my hairstyle, ultimately leading to a brave transition from chemical reliance to a more natural expression of who I was. As I shaved my head and embraced baldness, I slowly began reclaiming my identity.

In those early days, I wrestled with the idea of what it meant to have these illnesses. The fear of being viewed as weak crept into my mind like an unwelcome guest. I noticed the way people would occasionally look at me differently, as if the diagnosis was written on my face. This perception haunted me, and I struggled to push back against it. But I soon realized that the most significant challenge was not just how others viewed me; it was how I viewed myself.

It was during this tumultuous time that I found inspiration in the lives of the strong women around me. One person who truly impacted my perspective was a good friend I served with in the military who was battling multiple sclerosis (MS). Watching her handle her challenges was a marvel. Despite being bound to a wheelchair due to her condition, she radiated determination and resilience. I will never forget a conversation we had where she shared her longing to run just one more day. Hearing her heartfelt wish struck a chord deep within me. It was a sudden reminder of the blessings we often take for granted, like the simple joy of movement.

"I wish I could run just one more day," she said. I could see the unyielding desire in her eyes—the frustration of longing for physical capabilities denied to her now, a stark reminder that life can change in an instant. Her words brought a mix of sadness and inspiration; it was an awakening for me. The desire to be active and take my health for granted was something I had done for so long. I started to realize that I was wasting what I had, stressing over limitations rather than embracing the abilities I still possessed.

Her words ignited something within me. How could I allow a diagnosis to limit my potential when I witnessed her unwavering spirit? This realization marked a turning point. I understood that while I couldn't ignore my health challenges, I could shift my focus toward what I could still accomplish. Identity is more than just the labels we carry; it is shaped by our ability to navigate the storms life throws our way.

Another powerful influence in my journey was the wife of a good friend. She, too, faced an autoimmune disorder but lived life to the fullest. She is a remarkable woman. She's a dedicated mother, a supportive wife, and a passionate educator. Each day, she rises to the occasion, focusing on uplifting others while she battles her own health challenges. As I watched her travel, teach, and inspire countless people, I was left in awe. There she was, conducting workshops and igniting the spark of learning in her community, all while managing illness.

I couldn't help but compare our situations. How could she manage not only her health but also nurture those around her while I was struggling just to get out of bed? The shift in this comparison was crucial. Rather than let the difference in our journeys diminish my own, I gleaned motivation from her. I began to understand that it's not about magnifying the pains and limitations that come with a diagnosis; it's about adjusting my expectations and making space for a new version of thriving.

The change did not come easy. I had to confront my inner critic, the voice that berated me when I felt exhausted or limited. I remember one day when I had overexerted myself, trying to keep up with my old life. My body refused to cooperate, and I had to face the truth: I was tired. In those moments, I would get frustrated, calling myself weak for not being able to do what I once could. That voice echoed loudly—so loudly that I almost believed it. But I learned to silence it through kindness and grace.

While my friends' support was crucial, my family had a different impact—one that felt heavier and more complex. My youngest daughter faced challenges comprehending the invisible nature of my illness. How could she understand the fatigue and chronic pain I felt when all she could see was a bald spot on my head or the moments, I chose to curl up on the couch instead of joining her for a movie? She saw me "doing" things—going to work, attending events, being active—and couldn't fathom that these activities required an extraordinary amount of resourcefulness just to accomplish.

The more my daughters tried to comprehend my daily existence, the clearer it became that they were concerned for me but perhaps felt embarrassed as well. The youngest caught it bad at school when other kids teased her about her "bald" mom. She would defend me fiercely, sometimes even confronting other children who were unkind. I struggled with this deep parental desire to protect their feelings without dragging them into the despair of my illness.

There was a moment when my youngest confronted me after I had to back out of an outing due to exhaustion. Her disappointment mirrored my own, and it struck me that I had not only let myself down but my children as well. I realized I needed to be more open with them about what Sjogren's meant. I needed to explain that my feelings weren't always visible. This realization shifted my perspective; I learned that, as their mother, my role was to be resilient while also helping them understand that sometimes it is okay to not feel "normal."

Learning to give myself grace was perhaps the most significant change. It wasn't merely about accepting my limitations; it was about recognizing that I could still engage with life but in ways that honored my journey. I can't run like I used to or work long hours without feeling it later, but that's okay. I began to identify activities that could empower rather than deplete me. Instead of pushing against the tide of my health, I learned to navigate through it, using it as an opportunity to discover new passions, hobbies, and friendships.

With newfound inspiration, I started to reassess my limitations not as walls but as adjustments. Yet, the journey was not without its struggles. I found it difficult to let go of the old me—the hard charger who pushed through with relentless energy. Days would come when my body demanded rest, and in those moments, I battled against myself. Screaming voices in my head told me that if I couldn't do everything, I was being lazy. I bruised my own self-esteem, feeling like an imposter in my own skin.

Realizing that I needed to quit beating myself up was a significant turning point. I learned that insisting on pushing myself beyond what my body could handle was a form of self-sabotage. Accepting that I wouldn't be able to do everything the way I once did was a tough pill to swallow. But through this painful acceptance, I also discovered the importance of grace. Just because my body needed a different pace didn't mean I had to give up on my passions altogether.

I started incorporating small adjustments to my daily routine—like practicing self-compassion. Instead of pushing relentlessly through workshops and events, I learned to celebrate small victories. A half-day of teaching became a major win instead of a failure against my former self. I found that nurturing my well-being was crucial. This included carving out time for rest and recharging both my physical and mental batteries and allowing myself to partake in activities I love, albeit in a more manageable way.

Self-care became a priority. I engaged in activities that fulfilled me and rekindled that love for life I had as I acknowledged my contributions and strengths despite my changing circumstances. I began to let my story unfold, sharing my experiences with friends, family, and community members. This sharing forged authentic connections, where vulnerability opened the door to understanding and empathy.

Amidst my health challenges, I also looked to my friends battling even more severe ailments like cancer. Their unwavering determination motivated me to fight my battles, even on days I felt overwhelmed. If my friends could wake up daily with optimism, I could handle my challenges too. I began to adopt the mindset of "no weapon formed against me shall prosper"—a belief that helped fend off feelings of defeat and despair.

The power of community and family became my steadfast anchors. My daughters, while initially embarrassed, began to understand that their mom was still there for them, just in a slightly different way. They watched me fight through the fog of fatigue and pain. They learned that life would throw challenges our way, but that we could navigate those storms together. I hoped to be an example to them that they need not be defined or limited by their circumstances.

Every step I took toward resuming an active life sent ripples of positivity. I started to change my narrative: I was not a diagnosis; I was a mother, a friend, a worker, a fighter. I chose to keep living, to keep showing up, to keep pushing through on even the hardest days. I grasped the essence of resilience and self-acceptance. It dawned on me that being resilient means embracing your limitations without letting them overshadow your core self. Self-acceptance translates to valuing your worth beyond any diagnosis or transient condition.

I discovered empowerment as I shared my journey. While the experience of Sjögren's and alopecia was not one I ever signed up for, narrating my story helped others find their voices. And as they opened up about their struggles, a beautiful thread of solidarity began to weave through our conversations. I realized that by expressing our truth, we could support one another in profound ways.

For women facing similar health challenges who might feel lost, I have one piece of steadfast advice: surround yourself with supportive individuals. The relationships you nurture can become a lifeline. Always be kind to yourself and give yourself room to grow in your own way. Embrace the small victories; they matter. Every day may not be easy, but that doesn't mean we can't find light amid the darkness.

The changes in my relationships were noticeable. I started prioritizing those who genuinely supported me and backed away from those who questioned my health or dismissed my experiences. I still didn't get out much; with my job and responsibilities, there was little time for dating or socializing. It was a lonely place, but I found community in unexpected ways. Connecting with others at marathons and triathlons filled a part of me that had felt so disconnected when I was diagnosed. Everyone on that course had their own resilience stories, and their determination inspired me. Together, we celebrated achievements and offered encouragement, recognizing that we were all fighting our own battles.

Looking beyond my diagnoses, I began to see a clearer vision of my future. I knew the path forward would not be linear. My experiences had reshaped my understanding of burnout, identity crises, and how I fit into the larger tapestry of life. I aspired to use my journey not just as a means of healing but also as a source of motivation for others. I wanted them to see that they are more than their circumstances.

Emerging from the storm, I dream of a life filled with purpose and passion, engaging in advocacy to raise awareness about autoimmune diseases and empowering other women to find their strength in adversity. My diagnoses may have paved a rocky path, but they will never define who I am. Instead, they have created a story of resilience, a testament to the idea that we are much bigger than our challenges. Through everything, I now stand stronger, committed to writing this chapter of my life by embracing joy, sharing love, and inspiring others to shine through their own storms.

It's vital to remember that illness, whether it's a diagnosis like Sjögren's or alopecia, weighs differently on each person. They may not appear life-threatening in the traditional sense, but they're still challenges that deeply impact daily living. Their emotional and mental ramifications can be just as profound as those faced by someone diagnosed with more severe illnesses like cancer or MS. I learned that the comparison game only exacerbated feelings of defeat. What truly mattered was my struggle, which deserved space, compassion, and understanding.

Reflecting on my journey, I realized that I evolved significantly from the initial shock of my diagnosis.

Reflections on Growth

Instead of feeling defined by it, I found empowerment in my experience. I learned to communicate my limitations and educate those around me, including my co-workers and my daughter, about what Sjögren's disease is and what it means for me. I had to advocate for my boundaries and explain that my energy and health were not visible signs of my worth or capability.

This journey has taught me to advocate fiercely for myself, to seek medical professionals who respect my story, and to maintain a focus on who I am beyond my conditions. I refuse to let Sjögren's and alopecia define me. They are parts of my life, but they do not fully encompass who I am. Embracing the new reality means I had to make adjustments while still pursuing goals that matter to me.

Journaling became a sanctuary in my chaotic thoughts. It was there that I could express both my fears and my triumphs. Over time, I carefully crafted a vision of who I wanted to be, one that exceeded mere survival. I wanted to shine, even when storms raged around me.

Through these experiences, I have learned invaluable lessons. I realized that I wasn't limited to what my diagnosis could do to me. There was strength in vulnerability, and each time I took the brave step to share my story, I empowered not only myself but those around me too. My journey with Sjögren's helped illuminate the truth: we are larger than our struggles. Though our journeys may differ, the essence of who we are remains intact.

To every woman navigating a personal storm, know this: what you face does not define you. You are not a label, a diagnosis, or a limitation. You are a warrior, capable of fighting through the storms that life presents you. Find your inspiration, whether it be in others or within, and harness it. Understand that it's okay to stumble, to feel overwhelmed, and to seek support. You are bigger than the diagnosis.

With every battle I face, I emerge stronger. My story isn't finished, and yours isn't either. Embrace your journey; fight through the storms with gratitude for what you can do. It may take time, grace, and understanding, but you will come out victorious, shining brightly through the clouds. Do not let your diagnosis define who you are; you are capable of so much more. Step forward with courage and know that your light will shine through, no matter the storm.

As I look back on this chapter of my life, the biggest takeaway is clear: Don't let your diagnosis define you. You are bigger than what you're dealing with. Understand your challenges and create a new normal, but never stop pursuing your goals. It might be necessary to get creative or modify your plans, but you can still reach them. Embrace advocacy not just for yourself, but for those who might tread the same path. Let your experience be a bridge for others. The diagnosis is just a part of your journey, not the entire story. You have the power to write your own chapter amidst the storms of life.

Remember, at the end of the day, we are bigger than our diagnoses. They do not have to define us. Life is truly about showing up, not just for us but for those we love as well. As I continue this journey with Sjögren's disease and alopecia, I embrace every moment.

Moving Forward with Resilience

I encourage you to do the same: refuse to let your situation define who you are.

TIME 2 REFLECT; TIME 2 S.H.I.N.E.

"Action is the foundational key to all success." – Pablo Picasso

This isn't about what I've done—it's about what's possible when you choose to Spread Hope, Inspiration aNd Encouragement in your own life and the lives of others.

S - Spread Hope:

Think of a time when you faced something that left you feeling paralyzed, whether it was a diagnosis, a personal setback, or even a tough season of life. What gave you the strength to keep going?

H - Highlight Inspiration:

Who or what in your life has been a beacon of light when you felt like everything was dark? How can you bring that light back into your current situation?

I - Invest in Myself:

What's one small change I can make today that will help me take better care of my body, mind, or spirit? It doesn't have to be big—but it must be intentional.

N - Name My Truth:

What is something I've been afraid to admit to myself? It could be a fear, a limitation, or a desire. Write it down. The first step in moving forward is owning your truth.

E - Embrace the Journey:

How can I be kinder to myself in the middle of this? What would it look like to give myself grace when things aren't perfect?

CHAPTER 2

BALD, BOLD AND BECOMING

"Just shave it all off." Those four words hung in the air like a dare, echoing the tumultuous sea of emotions churning inside me. The clippers buzzed to life, a relentless hum that drowned out the self-doubt that had haunted my every reflection. As my hair fell away, so too did the weight of expectations—mine and everyone else's. This was not merely an act of defiance against alopecia; this moment was a catalyst, propelling me into a journey of fierce self-acceptance. I would soon discover that shedding my hair was just the first step toward uncovering the bold, radiant woman I had longs to be.

D-Day

The day I decided to shave my head was a turning point—like stepping off a cliff and discovering that the freefall is exhilarating. It wasn't a single leap into the deep end; instead, it was a gradual descent into a series of decisions—each one a step farther from the familiar comfort of having hair and closer to an unfamiliar territory where I could embrace baldness.

Over the years, I had tried so many hairstyles: from cute short cuts to trying out wigs and weaves. Nothing felt quite right. Eventually, I let my hair grow natural into what we lovingly call a "TWA," or teeny-weeny afro. But every time I looked in the mirror, I was reminded of the bald spots sneaking in like unwelcome guests.

After much consideration and countless trips to my barber, Mr. D, for fading cuts that still showcased my missing hair, I reached a breaking point. On June 22, 2022, I felt an overwhelming wave of frustration wash over me. Tired of stressing about my hair every single day, I told Mr. D, "Just shave it. Shave it all off." I remember thinking that if I didn't like it, I could cover up with a wig for scarves for a few weeks until it grew back.

Moment of Liberation

With the clippers humming, I felt a rush of relief. It was liberating. The moment Mr. D turned the chair around to face the mirror, I was met with my new reflection—a bald head shining brightly under the salon lights. Tears welled up in my eyes, not out of sorrow, but from a profound sense of empowerment. I was staring at someone bold, someone strong, someone I hadn't seen in a long time. It was a fresh canvas—one that was no longer tainted by my struggle, but rather, one that gleamed with potential and liberation.

I went home that night, a whirlwind of emotions, and celebrated my transformation with a full makeover—a personal "coming out" moment that felt like reintroducing myself to the world. I put on bold, bright lipstick, donned vibrant clothing that matched my newly found brazen spirit, and even staged a photo shoot to document the moment. It was cathartic, exhilarating, and for the first time in a long while, I felt beautiful.

Redefining Beauty

Shaving my head not only changed how I viewed myself, but it also altered my perception of femininity altogether. With the weight of my hair gone, I became acutely aware of the beauty that existed in baldness. I began noticing other women who had also embraced their baldness—they became my silent sisterhood. Each encounter with a bald woman in public sparked joy and connection. I found myself fist-bumping and complimenting them boldly: "You are beautiful!" Their beaming smiles and shared acknowledgment felt profound, as if we had unlocked an unspoken bond, transcending societal standards of beauty.

The evolution of my style didn't stop with my head. While my clothing remained largely unchanged—ever vibrant and colorful—I dove into big, bold earrings. They became a statement piece, drawing attention upward while my scalp became an emblem of strength. I began experimenting with shapes and colors, embracing a playfulness that matched my newfound confidence.

The Power of External Validation

Interactions with others became rich with possibilities. The response I encountered when I walked down the street was often surprising. Compliments flowed freely: "You are stunning!" strangers would say, often stopping in their tracks and beaming their approval. The best compliments came just before my weekly 'shave day,' when hair would begin to shadow my scalp—a sign I'd need to address it soon. The unexpected boost in confidence was transformative. Each compliment felt like a validation of my choice to shave my head, reinforcing the idea that I was more than just my hair; I was a person, worthy and beautiful.

New You, New Routine

Beyond superficial changes, the shaving experience taught me the importance of self-care. I learned to prioritize the health of my scalp, exfoliating it as carefully as I would my face. Retaining a smooth, shining, and healthy-looking bald head felt good, but it also required diligence. My mornings took on a new routine; what once required time consuming grooming rituals had become succinct. I found joy in the simplicity of showering, running my fingers across my smooth scalp, and reveling in the freedom of not having to curl, comb, or otherwise fuss over hair. I no longer spent hours at the beauty salon or felt the weight of my hair's unruliness. It was liberating.

Embracing My Decision

As I reflected on all of this, I realized something major: embracing baldness had far-reaching benefits. It not only saved me time and money in my daily routine, but it also emphasized the importance of self-love. I no longer worried about how I looked in the mirror. Instead, I focused on the woman looking back at me. I allowed myself to shine brightly from within, fostering a positivity that radiated to everyone around me.

People often commented on how bold I was, but in reality, the courage I gained came from accepting my baldness, not fighting it. The emotional and physical journey had been difficult, but I realized along the way that it wasn't merely about hair loss; it was an awakening to my inner beauty, a redefinition of self that echoed from within. Finally, I started to embrace and express who I am beyond the veil of hair.

But the journey didn’t stop there. Embracing my baldness demanded that I reflect deeply on inner beauty. At the beginning, I struggled with feelings of embarrassment; I worried about what people would think and how they’d react. I had to overcome those insecurities to find a sense of confidence that was mine alone.

One of my biggest challenges was explaining my baldness to others.

Breaking Down Barriers

I often found myself in situations where people assumed I had cancer—especially when I'd visit the cancer clinic for migraine infusion treatments. Instead of retreating in shame when they asked, I learned to confidently explain my condition, "No, I don't have cancer." Each interaction became a chance to educate and break down barriers, turning what could've been embarrassing into a conversation about alopecia.

Children, with their innocent honesty, were often the most curious. They would gaze at me, wide-eyed, breaking the silence with questions. "What happened to your hair?" they would ask, and instead of feeling embarrassed, I welcomed their curiosity. I would explain my alopecia, using it as an opportunity to educate, breaking down barriers one encounter at a time. Children don't have the same preconceived notions that we adults do. This openness became an opportunity to foster understanding and awareness about conditions like mine, and it was refreshing to see how easily kids accepted my bald head without making it a big deal.

Finding Strength in Sisterhood

It surprised me how liberating shaving my head was, granting me a new level of acceptance—not just for myself but for others as well. I began to form connections with others who were also dealing with hair loss. I joined online communities and support groups where we could share our stories and encouragement with each other. The bond was uplifting. Each time I would share my journey, another woman would approach me and share hers. Many were feeling trapped by their hair loss, wanting to find the same confidence but worried about how to begin.

I remember advising those women to be bold—to take the leap like I had. I encouraged them, saying, "If you don't like it, you can always wear your wig again. You just have to try it." It became clear to me that my baldness wasn't a loss; it was an opportunity—a chance to connect, inspire, and empower others who might be struggling with their own identity.

Yet, it was not without challenges. My relationships fluctuated, with some people struggling to accept my baldness. I recall one date with a man who wore his discomfort like a heavy coat. He seemed embarrassed to be seen with someone who was bald. His awkwardness only deepened my sense of fear and doubt. I, too, faced criticism, particularly from my younger daughter, who grappled with my new appearance. It was a moment that forced me to confront the societal shame linked with baldness—a harsh reminder of how frail acceptance can be.

However, with confidence came resilience. I discovered that when a woman exudes self-assurance, it has a ripple effect on those around her. The awkwardness melted into acceptance. I realized that after embracing who I was, I could stand firm in my truth and that this shift sparked courage in others to see beyond outward appearance.

The Journey Beyond Hair

If I had known earlier how freeing and empowering it would be to embrace my baldness, I would have made that decision so much sooner. The journey of self-acceptance was not just about losing hair; it was about gaining strength. It led me to understand that beauty does not stem from our hair or our outward appearances; it arises from the confidence we cultivate within ourselves. If you're losing hair or facing changes, be courageous and take those bold steps because at the end of the day, loving yourself is what truly matters. Allow your baldness to become a canvas for your own unique beauty—a statement reflecting a life of resilience, empowerment, and authenticity. Embrace who you are and let your inner beauty shine. And who knows? You just might inspire someone else along the way.

In this narrative of self-discovery, my hope is that readers sense the warmth of empowerment waiting on the other side of perceived imperfection. When you permit yourself to step beyond appearances, extraordinary revelations await.

Embrace your beauty. Stand bold in your truth. Let the world see you shine—bald, bold, and becoming your best self.

TIME 2 REFLECT. TIME 2 S.H.I.N.E.

"I can be changed by what happens to me. But I refuse to be reduced by it."– Maya Angelou

This isn't about what I've done—it's about what's possible when you choose to Spread Hope, Inspiration aNd Encouragement in your own life and the lives of others.

S – Spread Hope:
What have you learned about identity that you wish others knew?
How can you use your story to uplift someone struggling with self-image?

H – Highlight Inspiration:
Who has modeled boldness and confidence for you, especially in their physical appearance or authenticity?
What made them shine?
How can you begin to wear your boldness like a crown?

I – Invest in Myself:
In what ways have you overlooked your own self-worth or hidden your light?
What's one bold thing you can do to celebrate yourself—today?
Whether it's a new outfit, a photo shoot, or a journal entry declaring your beauty—do it for you.

N – Name My Truth:
What limiting belief have you held about your appearance?
What's something you've told yourself that no longer serves the woman you are becoming?

E – Embrace the Journey:
How can I be more present and patient with myself as I grow through this season.

CHAPTER 3

50 STATES, 13.1 MILES AT A TIME

A sudden burst of triumph flooded my senses as I crossed the finish line, my legs quivering beneath me. I raised my arms in victory, but inside, doubt nagged at my heart. What had I just accomplished? A marathon? The very idea seemed impossible a few months ago. My journey began in the chaos of a storm, where running transformed from a mundane task to a lifeline. As I battled through that final mile, I realized that this triumph was just the beginning, setting me on a path to chase half-marathons across all 50 states to heal my heart and spirit.

It wasn't just one thing that ignited the fire within me to run half-marathons across all 50 states and Washington, D.C. My journey began in 2005, a low point that felt like a storm raging inside me. Life had thrown relentless emotional challenges my way, and I was desperate for a way to manage my pain—a shift, a distraction, something to occupy my racing thoughts. As fate would have it, one ordinary day I stumbled upon a postcard in my mailbox. The message leaped out: "Hey, do you like to travel? Do you want to make an impact in other people's lives? If this sounds like you, come to our interest meeting."

Curiosity piqued, I decided to attend an interest meeting the postcard promoted.

Discovering New Goals

At the meeting, they talked about exciting trips to places like San Diego or Hawaii. However, the catch was unexpected: you had to fundraise and, more importantly, you had to run a marathon. A marathon? That sounded wild! I never pictured myself running one. Marathon runners seemed like super humans—definitely not like me. The thought of running 26.2 miles felt daunting and impossible. But at that moment, I was ready for a challenge, something different to pull me out of my emotional turmoil. I thought, "Why not?"

If anybody knows me, when I jump in, I am all in. So I worked hard to fundraise and attended training, clinics, long run sessions, soaking in all the information I could. The day of my first marathon came, and I was filled with nerves and excitement. It took me to a beautiful place called Kona. I completed the marathon, but I crossed that finish line vowing to never do it again. One and done, I declared. Or so I thought. But as life unfolds in unexpected ways, my journey was just beginning.

Years passed, and a change began to take root in my heart. I ended up working with a boss who was an absolute Run Disney fanatic. She shared stories about her weekend adventures running Disney races and came back proudly displaying shiny medals adorned with sparkling bling. I couldn't help but think, "That sounds amazing!" The lure of vibrant experiences began to call to me again.

Then I moved to a different assignment and met coworkers who were into running the Rock 'n' Roll races. At that time, I was living in Italy, and they offered events in places like Lisbon, Portugal; Madrid, Spain; Nice, France; Edinburgh, Scotland; and Oslo, Norway. Suddenly, running transformed for me from a dreaded chore into an adventure. It became my sanctuary. As a single mom with a demanding military job, I desperately needed an escape. These races allowed me to explore new cities one footstep at a time, while clearing my head in the process.

Running as a Healing Journey

Each race became an opportunity not just to compete but to heal. Fast forward again, and my connection with the running community blossomed. Meeting up with friends became my regular routine; we affectionately dubbed ourselves "RunFam." Together, we took on the Rock 'n' Roll Hall of Fame challenge, completing fifteen races in one year, motivated by the prospect of shiny bling and that inevitable sense of achievement.

This created a deeper drive within me. Competing, racing, and earning status as half fanatics and marathon maniacs became our shared identity.

While others leaned on the comfort of established routines, I decided on the audacious goal of finishing my 50-state challenge before I turned 50. The thought was daunting, filled with medical setbacks and challenges. Yet isn't life itself a continuous challenge? Each mile I ran became not only a step toward accomplishing that 50-state goal but also a step toward reclaiming my mental clarity amid the chaos of life.

You see, I've always been a runner at heart. Back in high school, I ran track, much to my surprise. I had been roped into joining the cross-country team by my enthusiastic coach, but it turned out to be a blessing. Whenever I faced stress or difficult emotions, running was my remedy. I would lace up my shoes and hit the pavement. With each stride, clarity washed over me. The worries of life seemed to dissipate, if only for an hour or so.

Running gave me peace. It let me connect with God and the world around me without distractions. After a good run, I would always feel better—really better, like I could conquer anything. It created a sense of euphoria known as a "runner's high." I realized quickly that when I didn't run, my mood dipped, and I became irritable. I felt broken at times, missing the joy that movement brought to my life.

As I continued to run through challenges, I came to realize that this journey was deeply therapeutic. Long runs allowed me time to think, to process what was happening in my life. When racing, I found confidence and strength I never knew I had. I often ran alongside many others, each with their own stories and struggles, proving to me that we all face challenges—some visible and some hidden.

The Impact of Community

The running community became my support system. It felt like having a team who cheered me on through every twist and turn. Their enthusiasm was infectious. I lovingly referred to this community as my "pimp or dealer"—once you get hooked into their energy and passion, it's hard to resist joining in on the next fun race or challenge. It amazed me how conversations around races could spark a fire in people, drawing them into a world where pain and exhaustion were invigoratingly transformed into something meaningful. In every race, whether a marathon or half-marathon, the air throbbed with enthusiasm and encouragement.

My RunFam helped me realize that it wasn't just about the races or chasing after medals; it was about the relationships we built. Everyone celebrated each other's victories, whether it was someone completing their first race or someone chasing their 500th medal. We cheered for each other, creating an atmosphere filled with love and camaraderie.

One race experience stands out—the race where I earned my Rock 'n' Roll Hall of Fame status. Reaching the Hall of Fame not only signified an accomplishment for me but also for others who looked up to me as an inspiration. I was one of the few African American females to achieve this, and it infused a sense of belonging and purpose into my running story. But like all heights, achieving that status left me longing for more. I yearned to chase the next challenge and embrace running's deeper transformation into my life—more than races and medals.

Achieving this status propelled me to reach for new challenges. Running became more than just a sport; it transformed into a journey of empowerment. I wasn't merely running for the sake of running anymore. Each mile I conquered brought a new realization that endurance was about more than just crossing the finish line; it was about how I spoke to myself during that journey, especially when no one was there to cheer me on.

Empowerment Through Running

Each state I entered I developed an intentional mindset. I learned resilience, presence, and the grit to keep going. Running taught me discipline: to create and maintain a routine, to budget effectively, to know when to rest and recover.

During every race, without fail, there were moments when my body screamed surrender. But it was in these moments God sent angels in the form of fellow runners—kind words and shouted praises instilling a strength I never knew existed within me.

Music became my companion on these journeys. Gospel songs would often turn my runs into joyous moments of praise, lifting my spirit further. There have been times when my heart raced not just from exercise but from incredible emotions that spilled over, shaping new perspectives during those runs.

I often encountered stirring experiences during races. One particularly poignant memory was during the Marine Corps Marathon, where we ran what was called the "memory mile." Lined with faces and names of fallen soldiers, their families cheered us on with flags held high. At that moment, life gained profound meaning beyond my individual struggles. I found clarity in understanding that life wasn't about the finish line but about the journey and the people who supported me along the way.

These emotionally charged experiences reshaped my understanding of resilience. Facing the brutal challenges alongside names I knew or sacrifices I felt in my heart transformed running into a mission. It became an act of service for those who faced greater adversities than I. I dedicated my races to those who could not run, either through circumstances or loss—people who inspired me in unspoken ways.

The Power of Dedicating Races

Dedicating my races gave each mile an enriched sense of purpose. I was no longer just running for myself but for those who fought invisible battles. It fueled my desire and pushed the limits of my endurance. I learned that getting started was often the hardest part, but pushing through difficult miles was the true test of will. Time and again, I watched others who faced physical hardship complete their races, which made my own struggles feel small in comparison. With each mile, I reminded myself that running is about more than competition; it's about community, empowerment, and unconditional support.

Through triumphs and setbacks, I learned motivation surfaces in unexpected ways. When sidelined from racing, I looked at the setbacks as temporary, concentrating on the possibility of healing and returning to my journey. I pushed myself through the pain, embracing rehabilitation diligently. My commitment had switched from just competing to remapping my goals on a vision board—seeing my dreams illustrated every day invigorated my spirit.

This tenacity pushed me to embark on my 50-state goal before 50, cementing my belief that healing doesn't always come with rest. Running, with all its trials and tribulations, became my medicine, my mission, my mindset. I learned that persevering meant nurturing my spirit, choosing empowerment over pain, and recognizing that limitations are self-defined.

Despite the many physical and emotional hurdles, I encountered, there was never a moment I was ready to give up. I didn't always feel strong; I felt broken, lost, and exhausted. Yet through the storm, I laced up my shoes, showed up, and kept moving.

I often reflected on how far I had come, remembering all the time and effort I poured into my goals. I chased my passion relentlessly, ensuring my commitments were met. This isn't just about crossing race finish lines. It's about running my race—even when no one is cheering me on. All of that was tested during one of my most challenging races.

Finding Strength in the Struggle

The Pikes Peak Ascent isn't just another race on the calendar—it's a rite of passage, a grueling test of grit and determination. Surrounded by towering pines and the scent of wildflowers, the air is thin, tainted with the reality that each breath comes laden with hardships and aspirations. As I laced up my shoes, doubt crept in like a chill on an early morning run. Could I really conquer this beast? Could I really make it to the summit, 14,000 feet above sea level, with only a half marathon's worth of distance to traverse?

The starting line buzzed with nervous energy. Runners exchanged quick smiles, knowing we were embarking on an odyssey that would stretch the limits of our minds and bodies. Could a mere 13.1 miles encapsulate the journeys of our lives—where every mile felt like its own struggle? As I tightened my laces, I recalled the turbulent transitions that had led me here: health challenges that left me questioning not just my body, but my identity; the burnout that came with balancing motherhood, career, and the ever-persistent shadow of self-doubt. Run, they said. Just run. But what if simply running could be a metaphor for something larger—an antidote to adversity?

The ascent began. Immediately, the inclines reminded me I was in for more than just an average race. Steep rocky paths beckoned, each unaided step hammering home the notion that I was not just climbing a physical mountain, but a metaphorical one, carrying the weight of my past and the hopes for my future with every push against gravity.

As I navigated the winding trails, bursts of encouragement from fellow racers flared up in puffs of oxygen. "You can do this!" became a mantra that echoed in my mind as I labored upwards, lured by the shimmering promise of the finish line. Just as life often pulls us into the deep end of the pool, I was pulled into the grip of fatigue and yearning for something more. I stared out at the breathtaking views and thought of the storms I'd weathered—health crises that felt insurmountable; transitions that knocked the wind from my sails. Each of those experiences echoed in the rhythm of my running.

The sun glimmered brightly, but it offered no warmth as my muscles burned with each uphill stride. I remembered how the journey of reclaiming my strength involved acknowledging the weariness that sometimes physically held me back. And yet, it was in that very acknowledgment that I found a flicker of resilience—not in sprinting toward a perfect finish, but in determined, steady steps. "One foot in front of the other, just like life," I whispered to myself.

Around the halfway point, I felt the strain building in my legs, heavy like the doubts that so often weighed down my spirit. They say that in endurance races, the hardest part is that moment when you realize how far you still must go, but I held fast to that inner flicker, that recognition of potential within. The irony of pursuing something extraordinary amid the ordinary—of each parched breath matching my parched spirit—reflected the harmony life often demands.

As I approached the final stretch of the race, the overwhelming altitude scraped the corners of my psyche, reminding me of the fragility of life's highs and lows. It was both daunting and humbling. I recalled stories of women who had pressed forward, even when they might've felt like they were crumbling from the inside out. I thought about the mothers I knew working tirelessly to balance everything while fighting battles under the surface; the women in my life who had grappled openly with their identities, often emerging stronger through their own mountains.

Then, with two minutes to spare, I reached the summit—a mere heartbeat from the edge of collapse. The moment surged with the joy of exhaustion and triumph. I crossed that finish line just in time, but all I could feel was the thumping of my heart as I collapsed, my energy drained to its last flicker. The medics rushed to me, oxygen in hand, but even in that disorienting state, I felt alive—more alive than I ever had in my life. Just then, through the haze, it became clear that each step—each carefully measured mile—wasn't just about running; it was about healing, about purpose, about confronting every trauma and fear with the courage to just keep showing up.

There is an undeniable power in movement, a unique blend of medicine and mindset. No, life won't wait for the perfect moment. Healing isn't a sprint but a slow, often painful climb, one step at a time. And while I may not have set out to conquer Pikes Peak perfectly, I displayed a resilience that circled back to my quest for clarity and purpose, redefining what it means to push forward.

Ultimately, what I learned that day—what I hope resonates with you—is that we all carry our storms, our burdens, and even our traumas. Yet within every tempest, there's an opportunity to transform. Every mile raced, each hill climbed, reminds us of our strength—and that with every intentional step, something extraordinary awaits.

Grateful Reflections

At the end of my journey across all 50 states, I realized that healing came through a most unexpected way—movement, mission, and mindset. My challenge of running half-marathons became so much more than a test of endurance; it led to profound spiritual and mental transformations. I learned that running across every state wasn't just about finishing races—it was about reclaiming my strength, choosing purpose over pain, and proving to myself (and others) that limitations don't define who I am—my perseverance does.

This chapter is my invitation for you to discover your own rhythm of resilience. Regardless of how lost you might feel within life's storms, I encourage you to lace up, show up, and take that first step toward your unique journey. It is in these steps, however small, that we realize our strength lies not in perfection but in our persistence, our willingness to reclaim our spirit, and—in the running journey of it all—our capacity to inspire others to join us in our courageous pursuits.

TIME 2 REFLECT. TIME 2 S.H.I.N.E.

"You don't have to run 13.1 miles to take back your power. Sometimes, just choosing to get up and keep going is the boldest race of all."- Tammy Dotson

This isn't about what I've done—it's about what's possible when you choose to Spread Hope, Inspiration aNd Encouragement in your own life and the lives of others.

S – Spread Hope:

Think of a time when you faced something that left you feeling paralyzed—maybe it was a diagnosis, a personal setback, or an unexpected season of loss.

What gave you the strength to keep moving forward when everything in you wanted to stop?

Who reminded you that you didn't have to stay stuck?

H – Highlight Inspiration:

Who or what in your life was a beacon of light when you felt surrounded by darkness?

A friend, a scripture, a song, a moment of clarity—what inspired you when your soul felt weary?

How can you bring that light into today's journey?

I – Invest in Myself:

This journey isn't just about going the distance—it's about "choosing yourself daily", even in the smallest ways.

What's one intentional change you can make today to take better care of your body, mind, or spirit?

Something simple, but healing—like stretching, hydrating, journaling, or simply breathing deeply in gratitude.

N – Name My Truth:

What's something you've been afraid to admit to yourself? A fear? A dream you've buried? A lie you've believed about what you're capable of?

Write it down. Speak it. Own it. Truth brings freedom.

E – Embrace the Journey:

The road won't always be smooth, but your story isn't less powerful because it's messy.

How can you be kinder to yourself today?

What does it look like to run your race with grace—even if you have to walk sometimes?

CHAPTER 4

SINGLE, STRONG, AND STILL SHOWING UP

As the sun dipped below the horizon, casting a golden hue across the chaos of my living room, I felt the weight of expectation crashing down. Juggling a demanding career in the military, nurturing my daughters, and holding onto my dreams was like trying to balance on a tightrope suspended in a storm. In those vulnerable moments, the exhaustion framed by guilt wrapped around me like a heavy blanket, making me question if I could truly conquer this whirlwind. But it's in the tempest of demands and responsibilities that I found a flicker of hope—a realization that I wasn't alone. What would unfold in this chapter isn't just my battle; it's a heartfelt journey of resilience, community, and the unquenchable strength we uncover within ourselves as single mothers.

Essential Support Systems

Support systems are absolutely critical for single mothers, especially for those navigating the complexities of life while pursuing careers, health, and personal dreams. My journey, as a single mother who balanced a demanding military career with the emotional and logistical challenges of parenting, has taught me that help isn't just a bonus; it's a lifeline.

In a military environment, where assignments can shift unpredictably, and duty often calls during the most critical times, relying on a support system is not only necessary; it's essential. I vividly recall nights when my daughters needed care while I was stationed at work for extended hours, often overnight. During temporary assignments, known as TDYs, the demands of my job eclipsed my availability at home, making it imperative to have people I could trust to step in.

It's bittersweet to reflect on this aspect of my journey. My oldest daughter has spent more days with other families than with me, a reality that many single mothers may resonate with. Yet, through these experiences, I have discovered the cornerstone of resilience: the power of community and the myriad of individuals who silently shoulder the weight of our struggles.

Many single mothers find themselves in similar situations. They are often left without a traditional support system—absent partners and scattered families leaving a profound vacuum. I experienced this firsthand, with neither of my daughters having their fathers present in their lives. Family, too, was not as accessible as I had hoped. I was fortunate to have my older sister nearby and, more recently, my father, who stepped in much after his retirement. However, the bulk of my support has come from friends and community members.

Thinking back to the times when I had to deploy or undertake remote assignments, I recall the mix of fear and gratitude. I've learned to ask for help—even if it doesn't come in the form I envision. When trusting others, especially in caring for my children, I've leaned on a few close families within our church community. They opened their homes to my daughters as their own, providing comfort and stability during turbulent times.

As any single mother can attest, this reliance on external support comes with its own challenges. At times, asking a friend to care for your child feels burdening. I struggled with it constantly. Yet, it became increasingly clear that I could never do this alone. I've had moments where I had no choice but to place my daughters in the care of others for months at a time—a challenging reality that many single parents might face.

Balancing Priorities

Then there's the constant competing for time and attention amidst myriad responsibilities. How do you ensure to honor connections with your children while juggling career goals and health issues? I've often fallen short in this domain, feeling the weight of the "best mom ever" title slipping through my fingers during moments when I simply couldn't be there.

Reflecting on my journey, one thing stands out: communication. I learned, albeit later than I wish, that creating a healthy dialogue with my children about expectations, responsibilities, and limitations is crucial. Being introduced to personality assessments helped me recognize the different communication styles of my daughters and my own as a parent, guiding me to foster deeper understanding. When I fell short, I let my children know it was not due to a lack of love; I did my best for them with the tools I had at the time.

Through those early years, I aimed to ensure that my daughters engaged in sports and activities that excited them. I understood the importance of being present during those formative moments—the graduations, the sports events, and even the little victories. Even when my commitments took me away during holidays, I made sure to communicate the situation beforehand. It was important for me to be there for them, and in the rare instances I couldn't be, I tried to make those moments count.

Serving and Self-Care

Embracing the military motto "service before self" has been another double-edged sword in my life that has shaped both my ability to serve others and my self-care journey. This principle, while noble, is easily misunderstood in today's conversation about self-care. Early in my military career, I prioritized the needs of others, often at my own expense. This led to burnout, unfulfilled expectations, and regrets about the sacrifices made that affected my relationships with my children.

When it came time for me to consider my own health, especially during hospital stays and surgeries, I discovered how crucial it is to set boundaries and allow myself the time to heal. I had a profound realization: to care for others effectively, I must first care for myself.

Lessons in Vulnerability

However, that balance of self-care against the instinctive desire to meet everyone else's needs is delicate. In the depths of overwhelming feelings where tasks seem insurmountable, I've found respite not in what I can achieve but in recognizing what I cannot control. Finding clarity in the chaos has been an evolution of understanding the things I can manage—like allowing extra time for appointments or understanding that resilience often lies in acceptance of external factors, like traffic.

Among my worst habits, I've grappled with being an over-committer. Well, let's just say it's a lethal flaw. I have read every book under the sun about time management and prioritization. However, I still sit at my desk, faced with a daunting to-do list and the heavy realization that I am still a work in progress. When overwhelmed, the inclination to shut down is strong, but addressing the negative feelings head-on with helpful coping mechanisms like physical activity, counseling, and solidarity with friends kept me afloat.

Sacrifices, Sacrifices

Sacrifices have been the hallmark of my life—a tapestry woven with threads that are both rich and bittersweet. Having my oldest daughter at 22 instilled responsibilities that I couldn't see then but readily embrace now. Now, as I navigate raising my youngest, who presents an entirely different set of challenges, I sometimes ponder whether my sacrifices have led to missed connections with both of them. I see the contrast in our experiences, and I can't help but feel that I might have loved them more had I set aside the overwhelming claims of motherhood's demands.

The reality is that being a single parent, especially while pursuing a career, is about compromise. It means understanding the lasting impact of those choices. For every opportunity I've seized, there've likely been moments lost with them. Have I made the right choices? That question lingers in my mind, but what gives me peace is the knowledge that I did what I had to do with the resources at hand.

Feeling alone amidst the juggling act is not just an occasional sentiment; it's a frequent reality. In those quiet moments of solitude, the longing for support looms large. Learning to ask for help is easier said than done. Yet, looking back, I see how vulnerability allowed me to connect with angels disguised as friends who showed up just when I needed them.

As I've navigated the valleys of loneliness and weariness, I learned to appreciate unexpected gifts—kind messages from friends, encouraging encounters during physical activity—reminders of the community's support. Every time I reached out, people were willing to lend a hand. None of us can traverse this journey alone, and those relationships often come through when we least expect them.

Redefining Strength

Ultimately, the overarching truth I've learned is that strength is not the absence of struggle; it's the decision to keep showing up. Motherhood is not a flawless equation filled with perfect balance; it's an intricate dance of alignment with a purpose amidst chaos.

For every single mother reading this, remember: You are not alone in your weariness, your guilt, or your longing to get it "right." You may to feel stretched thin, but you can still live with purpose. Exhaustion does not negate effectiveness. You can show up imperfectly and still shine, embodying resilience and grace even when your resources feel depleted. Your challenges do not define you; courage shows up in moving through the storms with faith, even when the winds threaten to sweep you away.

Like me, you might grapple with how to define your strength and what grounds your purpose in the frenetic pace of life. Lean into your community. Seek out those pathways that allow you to rediscover your sense of purpose. When your vision aligns with those core values, you can navigate life's complexities without losing sight of your dreams.

Remember, balance may be elusive, but alignment is within reach when you approach life with intention. Embrace the notion that amidst the chaotic times, grace will carry you through challenges, reminding you that showing up is a form of strength.

TIME 2 REFLECT. TIME 2 S.H.I.N.E.

"You are stronger than you know, braver than you believe, and more loved than you can imagine." — A.A. Milne

This isn't about what I've done—it's about what's possible when you choose to Spread Hope, Inspiration aNd Encouragement in your own life and the lives of others.

S – Spread Hope:

Think about a time when you were stretched thin—giving everything to everyone else and wondering if there was anything left for you.
What reminded you that your presence, not perfection, is what truly matters?
Who do you know right now that might need a reminder of that same truth?

H – Highlight Inspiration:

Who has shown up for *you* when you felt like crumbling?
How did their strength or support shape your perspective on resilience and grace?
Take a moment to reflect on how God has used people, even in quiet ways, to help carry your load.

I – Invest in Myself:

You can't pour from an empty cup.
What's one way you can refill your emotional, spiritual, or physical tank this week?
Give yourself permission to *be* before you continue to *do*.

N – Name My Truth:

What expectation have you been carrying that no longer serves you—whether it's being "supermom," "unbreakable," or "always on"?
Write it down. Then give yourself grace to redefine what strength looks like in this season.

E – Embrace the Journey:

You're not just surviving—you're becoming.
In what ways has your motherhood (single or otherwise) journey made you softer, stronger, wiser, or more compassionate?
Celebrate that growth today.

CHAPTER 5

IRON WILL, IRON WOMAN

With the finish line looming ahead, my body feels like a detached entity, worn and weary from the grueling miles behind me. The voice inside my head shifts from encouragement to desperation, fighting against the overwhelming weight of fatigue: "This is too much."

But just as doubt threatens to overtake me, I hear the chant swell from the crowd—a united force shattering my fears. "Tammy Dotson, you are an IRONMAN®!" The words explode within me like fireworks, igniting an avalanche of emotions—joy, relief, and an immense gratitude for the journey and the people who made it possible. This moment isn't just the end of a race; it's the start of a profound realization about the indelible strength found in community and the power of pushing through life's storms.

Crossing the finish line of an IRONMAN® is not just a physical achievement; it's an emotional tsunami of thoughts and feelings that washes over you like a wave after a long, exhausting race. As you sprint down that red carpet, the cheers of voices merge into one grand announcement: "Tammy Dotson, you are an IRONMAN®!" At that moment, a profound sense of relief surges through you, casting aside the burdens you may have carried for months. Tears stream down your face as joy fills your heart. It's like a heavy weight lifts off your shoulders, leaving you bathed in gratitude and pride.

Training for an IRONMAN® is no small feat; it's a monumental challenge that tasks every ounce of your physical, mental, and emotional resolve. It is a journey steeped in resilience, faith, and an unwavering commitment to push past your limits. Imagine swimming 2.4 miles, cycling 112 miles (and in my case it was 116 miles), and then running a full marathon of 26.2 miles—all in a single day!

But for me, it wasn't only about proving I could do these physically demanding tasks. It was about something deeper—about resilience, faith, and the strength I discovered within myself. My own journey to the IRONMAN® began not as a straightforward athletic goal but as a recovery process marked by determination and hope after facing significant health challenges. The hardest battles, I discovered, were not only fought on the physical plane but deeply rooted in the mind and spirit.

The Birth of a Goal

I remember vividly the moment I decided to train for the IRONMAN®. After undergoing major abdominal surgery in December 2019 and an open craniotomy in March 2020, my life had been substantially altered. Returning to form after serious medical interventions is not merely about rehabbing muscles; it's about rebuilding faith in yourself and your body's capabilities. The goal to complete a full IRONMAN® wasn't born out of the desire to achieve athletic prowess, but rather the need to reclaim a sense of agency in my own life. Training became my meditation, my prayer. Resilience is built one mile, one prayer, one choice at a time.

Preparing for an IRONMAN® is akin to preparing for a marathon of life itself. As I dove headfirst into rehabilitation, I curated a training schedule that would test my limits but also reaffirm my progress. Consistency was crucial. Early on, I embraced the bitter realities of training; the oppressive Florida heat, the thunderstorms that seemed to plague every long ride, and the emotional battles that raged within. The pursuit of my IRONMAN® goal demanded that I commit wholeheartedly, understanding that anything worth achieving is rarely easy.

There were days that I faced deep mental and emotional barriers; my body would remind me of the surgeries and the traumas I had endured. At times, it felt insurmountable. The echoes of "What do you think you're doing?" would flood my mind after particularly grueling workouts. Yet, those very doubts served as fuel to my resolve. I had tasted failure; my first attempt at a half IRONMAN® had ended in disappointment. I barely completed my second attempt, a testament to half-hearted training. Knowing I needed to respect the process gave me the clarity to push forward.

As I began to gain momentum and see results, my resilience steadily grew. There were, however, days when I questioned my sanity. "What was I thinking?" I pondered after a long training session where every part of me ached. Despite the doubts, the act of simply putting one foot in front of the other became a source of strength for me. It was at these moments that I leaned on my "why"—the fundamental reason I wanted to tackle this challenge. Why do we do anything we do? I realized I wanted to inspire others, to show them that the impossible could be achieved through faith and perseverance.

Faith played a monumental role in my journey. An IRONMAN® slogan says, "Anything is possible," but for me, my personal motto was, "With God, all things are possible." Each day, I prayed for strength, health, and guidance and started each morning with gratitude—a simple prayer acknowledging my existence and my health. "Thank you, Lord, for waking me up this morning, for giving me strength." Acknowledging the power of faith in my training was profound. I understood that many people doubted my capability, and those doubts only fueled my passion to prove them wrong. Whenever I faced setbacks, my faith rekindled my fire, allowing me to persevere when the strength I had physically seemed to wane.

My days were often a mental duel against the perceived impossibility of my journey, but moments of prayer rejuvenated my spirit, reminding me of my deeper purpose.

Witnessing others cross their finish lines amid downpours and chaos ignited a fire in me. With every inspiring victory I saw, my internal mantra solidified: "If they can do it, so can I." It is incredible how the success of others can illuminate our paths, but only if we allow ourselves to be inspired rather than intimidated.

The camaraderie with fellow racers creates a unique energy throughout the event. While each person may have individual goals—some aiming for the podium, and others just hoping to finish—the shared mission brings everyone together. Imagine the scene: dozens of swimmers rising to the challenge, cyclists battling the hills, and runners encouraging each other to keep pushing through the pain. There's an undeniable strength found in this collective spirit, one that you may not even realize existed within you until you're faced with the monumental task ahead.

Being surrounded by other participants is electrifying. It's not about competing against one another; instead, it's about a unified goal. Everyone is there for the same reason, albeit with different aspirations. For those not racing to be the fastest, every single athlete is a teammate in this journey, navigating their own trails of sweat and determination. You witness others pushing their limits, and it inspires you to dig deeper within yourself. When fatigue threatens to overpower your will, the collective energy pulsating in the air fills you with an almost supernatural strength.

Embracing Discomfort

As I neared race day, excitement mingled with anxiety. The water was my greatest fear; the swim leg of the IRONMAN® felt like a baptism by fire. It is daunting to know that if you fail at the swim, your day is over before it begins.

The adrenaline coursed through my veins as I lined up at the starting point, the cacophony of voices around me merging into a single hum of anticipation. As the horn blared, signaling the start of the IRONMAN®, I stepped forward, plunging into the water alongside hundreds of others—all of us strangers yet united in purpose. This was not just a race; it was a testament to human spirit.

In the frigid embrace of the water, it struck me how often we, especially as women navigating our personal storms, fight battles that transcend physical constraints. We are warriors in our daily lives, and simultaneously being a part of a collective with a shared goal resonates deeply. There's a profound strength that emerges from camaraderie, an invisible line connecting us amidst the chaos of competitive instinct.

Every stroke I took in that water was more than just a movement; it was a declaration—that I, too, belonged in this space. I was not merely a body moving through water; I was a soul grappling with doubts and fears, transformed into a force of nature by the unyielding support of my fellow competitors. It was staggering to acknowledge how much of our potential we camouflage beneath layers of self-doubt. Yet, in that moment, as I navigated the currents, I felt an almost supernatural strength, a hidden reservoir of resilience surfacing with each movement.

Yet, the swim turned out to be a surprising symphony of calm amidst chaos. I emerged on the other side invigorated, a testament to the inner strength I had been nurturing through each training session.

As I exited the water and transitioned to the bike, another wave of emotions surged through me. The comfort of knowing that my fellow participants and I shared the common goal of endurance—this was a collective mission. We were not opponents; we were allies pushing each other forward, creating an environment that was empowering and uplifting. Each turn of the pedals became a symbol of perseverance, of leanings into discomfort, the essence of deeply embedded resilience.

While the faster competitors focused on podium placements, I found my strength not just within myself, but in the journey of those like me—those who weren't just racing against the clock but battling their own limitations. These were the participants for whom every second counted; for whom crossing that finish line within a 17-hour time limit was an achievement far greater than any medal could denote. Their determination bolstered my own, igniting an unshakeable resolve within me.

Then came the bike leg. A deluge of rain, wind, and unrelenting sun greeted me—a surreal representation of life itself. I had encountered every imaginable condition during training, so when the storm hit during the race, I was both prepared and grateful. If I had learned anything from my journey, it was that success is often found not in the avoidance of adversity but in the effective navigation through it. The roads were littered with those sidelined by bike mishaps and emotional breakdowns. However, I felt the confidence borne from all those training rides, even in less-than-ideal conditions.

After hours of gravel, sweat, and silence punctuated by the sounds of nature, I faced the run—a daunting 26.2 miles waiting to test my spirit. Unlike the previous sections where physical might felt predominant, this run unfolded into a journey of soul-searching. The miles melted away as I focused entirely on each step I took. I was a woman chiseled from iron, reborn with every passing moment. The cheers of the crowd became an anchor in the tumultuous waves of challenge, lifting me through fatigue.

Then it happened. About six miles into the run, a sharp, crippling pain shot through my knee; it was as if my body had issued an ultimatum. I went down, excruciating pain seizing me. Panic coursed through my veins at the idea of not finishing what I'd fought so hard to start. Thoughts of giving up flickered in my mind. But there was no quit in me, only a deep-rooted sense of determination. In the shadow of despair, I found clarity. No team would finish this race without each other. I was not alone on this journey.

That's when I met Kevin, a fellow IRONMAN® trainee. He was hunched over in absolute agony from back spasms, and we looked at each other as kindred spirits stranded in difficulty. We encouraged each other to keep moving, our shared determination turning pain into power. Together, we formed a unique coalition, reminding one another that each step was still a step toward that coveted finish line.

I iced my knee, and though I could only walk for much of the remaining 20.2 miles, I had grit going for me. My fellow racers and I became a ragtag coalition; we cheered for one another even when we had nothing left to give.

In those dark moments when I felt defeated, I relied on positive affirmations, reminding myself of everything I had overcome. I couldn't have headphones on the course, so I created my own mental soundtrack, reciting empowering words that propelled me forward. "Come on, Tam! You got this!" became my personal cheerleading phrase, a reminder that my strength was deeper than I had ever believed.

I kept my eyes on the finish line. Each bead of sweat, every glimmer of exhaustion, fueled my determination. Significant ramifications surged through me—I did not just want to finish; I NEEDED to finish. Pure grit kept my mind focused. I had invested too much—physically, emotionally, and financially—to turn back now. I didn't want to let my coach or anyone who had supported me down, nor did I want to walk away without that coveted finisher medal. I wanted to solidify the transformation that had been occurring within me.

Crossing the Finish Line

As you make your way across the finish line, it's more than just finishing a race; it's a celebration—of resilience, personal triumph, and most importantly, teamwork. Many of the participants are on the course for hours longer than the elite athletes, pushing through grueling challenges but refusing to give up. Their grit teaches you a lesson about endurance and fortitude that extends well beyond the athletic realm. You realize that finishing isn't always about speed; sometimes, it's about sheer willpower and the relentless pursuit of your goals.

Crossing that finish line was transformative. As I staggered down the iconic red carpet, I was greeted by exhaustion and elation. That moment encapsulated every struggle, every prayer, and every ounce of sweat shed in training. When I stepped over the line, it felt as if a wave of everything I had overcome rolled off my shoulders. In that moment, I became not just a finisher of the IRONMAN®, but a testament to what resilience, faith, and determination can achieve. I had become someone new, reshaping the narrative of my life not just around illness but around triumph.

Crossing that finish line was not just a brutal physical challenge or athletic achievement; it symbolized a monumental transformation. It was proof that we could all conquer our personal storms. As I stood there, bolstered by a team comprised of doctors, therapists, coaches, and my unwavering Sherpa who sacrificed countless hours to support my endeavor, I recognized the beauty of collaboration and shared joy. My success was not merely mine; it was built on the backs of those who believed in me when I struggled to believe in myself.

This experience was a microcosm of life's greater truths. It mirrored the way we tackle challenges, navigate pain, and battle through chaos. The road to completion may seem daunting, yet it becomes navigable through collective effort, boundless support, and a fierce belief in the possibilities that lie within us. Emotional catharsis is often served on that very finish line—and for many, it marks the beginning of new aspirations.

Lessons Beyond the Race

At that moment, a profound understanding settled in: completing the IRONMAN® reinforced that I could achieve anything I set my mind to—if only I had the right support, resources, and guidance. This challenge ignited a flame within me that pushed boundaries I never thought possible. As the emotional rush subsided, I grasped the far-reaching implications of my experience.

The finish line, an entity often perceived as a destination, morphed for me into a mindset, shining the spotlight on personal goals and the limitations we inadvertently impose upon ourselves. Each barrier that seems insurmountable can be nudged aside with determination, courage, and, most importantly, an acknowledgment of community. I learned that just as I need my Sherpa to aid and motivate me, I too can be the beacon of support for someone else navigating their own tumult.

As I delved deeper into the essence of preparation—not just physically, but also mentally and emotionally—I recognized a universal truth: challenges, whether athletic or otherwise, are both intimate and communal. They teach us resilience and the importance of having a support system. The grit required to face an IRONMAN® is akin to what women face in their everyday storms. Both demand the same depth of faith, grit, and perseverance, underscoring that strength can be sourced from community as much as from within.

This journey taught me that the finish line is not merely a physical place but a mindset, an embodiment of resilience and belief. It's a mission to become the person God sees in you—the version of yourself capable of surmounting life's obstacles.

Reflections on Training

Anyone considering a similar athletic challenge must recognize that the pursuit of greatness requires discipline, discomfort, and deep faith. Understand your "why" and keep it at the forefront of your mind. In moments of doubt, remind yourself that you are capable of so much more than you realize.

Here are some tips for those who dare to tread this path:

1. **Set Clear and Meaningful Goals:** Why do you want to achieve this challenge? Keeping your reason close to your heart can fuel your motivation on tough days.

2. **Commit to Consistency**: Build a training schedule you can realistically follow. Don't be afraid to stretch yourself but ensure you're building a sustainable practice.

3. **Embrace Your Journey:** Your path will be unique, often filled with setbacks. Accept every twist and turn as part of your story; resilience grows through these trials.

4. **Focus on the Journey, Not Just the Destination**: Enjoy the process of training. Celebrate small victories along the way, not just the finish line.

5. **Seek Community:** Find a support system. Surrounding yourself with encouraging friends or training partners can make a significant difference.

6. **Engage Your Support System**: Share your goals with those around you. Their encouragement will bolster your resolve.

7. **Practice Positive Self-Talk**: During challenging moments, remind yourself of how far you've come. It's incredible the power words have over our psyche.

8. **Know Your "Why"**: Remind yourself constantly of the purpose behind your challenge. Solidifying your motivation will sustain you through tough times.

9. **Don't Fear Failure**: Embrace it as a glorious teacher. Every setback holds lessons that fortify your resolve to rise and try again.

10. **Be Kind to Yourself**: Acknowledge that the journey will be filled with struggles and embrace them. Growth often requires discomfort.

11. **Have Faith**: Lean into your convictions and let them empower you to reach heights beyond your imagination.

12. **Reflect and Recharge:** Carve out time for reflection throughout your journey. Understanding your mental and emotional landscape can help you navigate challenges ahead.

For those considering similar athletic challenges, my advice is simple yet monumental. Start by setting a date—today. Choose your race and dive headfirst into planning. Consider logistical aspects like location, difficulty, and environment deliberately. Secure an early registration to alleviate stress later on.

Once you've locked down your race, find a coach—someone who can challenge and guide you through the intricacies of training, helping to solidify your foundation and pushing you beyond perceived limits. Finding someone knowledgeable in your target area can spell the difference between simple training and a breakthrough experience. This person will challenge you, keeping you accountable, and allow you to grow stronger physically and mentally.

Equip yourself with a structured training plan, inclusive of nutrition practices for both training and race day, ensuring you remain both physically and mentally prepared.

Moreover, It's important to talk to your family about your commitment and assure them that you will dedicate time to this challenge. Their understanding and support grant you the freedom to pour your heart into your training without fear of disappointing them.

Share your journey, your challenges, and your aspirations. Their support can be transformative, alleviating the burden of isolation that sometimes accompanies intense training.

In training, allow your journey to be one of joy as well as labor. Following a training plan—blending strength training to support endurance, swimming skills, cycling techniques, and running strategies—is vital. Focus on each discipline in isolation, giving it your full attention, leaning into the rhythm of your training.

Observe how your body responds. Listen to its needs, admitting when fatigue demands rest. Celebrate your achievements through incremental goals, reminding yourself constantly that this journey requires mental tenacity as much as it does physical endurance. Staying healthy is imperative as you approach race day.

As you enter the final phases of your training, the mental game becomes just as crucial as the physical. You remind yourself: "I can do hard things."

On the day itself, instead of viewing the race with trepidation, you see it as a party—a day to celebrate all the hard work you've poured in. You compartmentalize your focus, concentrating solely on completing one leg at a time. The swim is your immediate mission, and once accomplished, you give your full attention to the bike. Finally, when you settle into a comfortable rhythm on the run, your spirit lifts with the realization that the finish line is within reach.

As you near the end, a swell of emotion builds within you. This isn't simply about finishing a race. It's about all the moments that led you here, all the struggles, the sacrifices, and the supportive hands that lifted you time and again. Crossing the finish line is just as much an ending as it is a beginning—a moment of becoming.

The IRONMAN® was not just a race; it was a metamorphosis. I entered the water one person, plowed my way through self-doubt and physical pain, and emerged transformed. Every runner, every athlete, every woman conquering her unique storm can harness that same resilience to find strength in adversity. You are capable of more than you think; you simply need to strive for it. Your finish line awaits on the horizon; recognize that it represents a moment of becoming that will transcend any athletic achievement.

As you stand at the precipice of your finish line, remember—you are capable of achieving extraordinary feats, yet every achievement will require moments of vulnerability, discomfort, and deep faith. The finish line isn't merely a physical place; it's a mindset, a mission in becoming the best version of yourself.

So, lace up your running shoes, embrace the challenges, and embark on your own path of self-discovery. Your journey awaits, filled with the promise of resilience, the thrill of camaraderie, and the powerful realization that you hold within you an unbreakable iron will. The race may begin with a step, but it culminates in a movement—a personal revolution. Your personal storm may intensify with the challenge, but as you cross your finish line, you too will be able to look back and say, "I am capable of more than I ever believed." Embrace it. Your moment is here.

TIME 2 REFLECT. TIME 2 S.H.I.N.E.

"Strength doesn't come from what you can do. It comes from overcoming the things you once thought you couldn't."— Rikki Rogers

This isn't about what I've done—it's about what's possible when you choose to Spread Hope, Inspiration aNd Encouragement in your own life and the lives of others.

S – Spread Hope:

Think about a time when you faced a mountain-sized challenge—something that felt beyond your strength.
What helped you push forward when giving up felt easier?
Who around you might need to know it's okay to start small, as long as they start?

H – Highlight Inspiration:

Who has modeled mental toughness or spiritual strength in your life?
What did they teach you—through words or actions—about perseverance and purpose?

I – Invest in Myself:

Endurance begins with daily discipline.
What's one commitment—big or small—you can make to challenge your body, focus your mind, or strengthen your faith this week?
Don't wait for perfect conditions. Start training your "inner athlete" now.

N – Name My Truth:

What limiting belief or excuse have you allowed to shape your choices?
Write it down. Then declare one truth from God's Word that cancels it out.
This is your mindset shift moment.

E – Embrace the Journey:

Growth often comes disguised as struggle.
How can you reframe your current challenge as a training ground—not punishment, but preparation?
What would it look like to finish well, no matter how long or tough the course?

CHAPTER 6

THE MORNING I COULDN'T MOVE

With every ounce of strength siphoned away, I lay there, evaluating my life's choices as shadows swirled and danced around me. My heart raced wildly, a drum of vulnerability resonating within the stillness of my room. This was more than just an aching body; it was a critical juncture—a breaking point where my past expectations collided violently with my present reality. The voice of my inner critic raged on, but beneath the tempest, a whisper emerged: it's time to stop fighting against the storm and start navigating its depths. In that moment of vulnerability, I began to understand that survival may not lie in incessant motion, but rather in the trembling act of stillness.

Not An Ordinary Morning

The moment I woke up, it felt as if I had just been in a car crash; my head throbbed mercilessly, and the searing pain coursed through my legs, igniting a fire that stretched from my feet all the way to my hips. As I lay there, the familiar sensation of desperate fatigue enveloped me, a weight heavier than lead pressing down on my body. I attempted to sit up, to force my eyes to focus on the familiar surroundings of my bedroom, but my legs—those stubborn appendages—felt like logs, unyielding and unresponsive. Panic brushed against the edges of my mind. Had I pushed myself too hard? Had I gone too far this time?

I was, lying in bed, confusion and fear creeping into the corners of my mind. **Why couldn't I move?** My heart beat loudly in my ears, thudding like a drum against the quiet of the room, a stark reminder of my vulnerability. Every part of me ached.

I closed my eyes, willing the chaos in my body to subside. I took deep breaths, hoping this moment of stillness would bring relief. But instead of drifting into comfort, I found myself trapped in a cycle of thoughts—the churning emotions spinning wildly within me. **What was happening?** The fear and frustration began to swirl inside me like a tempest. Every second spent lying there was a reminder of the person I used to be: the energetic, unstoppable version of myself who thrived on caffeine and barely any sleep. Somehow, that person seemed like a distant memory, lost to the whirlwind of chronic pain and exhaustion that had become my everyday reality.

I stumbled toward the bathroom, each step a monumental effort, only to be met with the realization that there was no victory in that act. My body betrayed me as I collapsed back into bed, the room spinning with every flicker of light. This catastrophic morning was not an isolated incident; it was the culmination of months of stress, fatigue, and a relentless amalgamation of this immune disorder, Sjögren's disease, that I had learned to navigate but not conquer.

An hour passed, but it felt like an eternity. I tried again. I had to get up—I needed to just get to the bathroom, but my legs betrayed me once more. The act of getting out of bed seemed monumental, as if I were attempting to move a mountain with sheer willpower alone. The realization crashed over me like a wave; I was not just physically unable to get up—I was emotionally stricken, beaten down by my body's refusal to cooperate.

The Voices Within

But as the storm raged within, there was also a whisper—a quiet voice in the chaos. **Listen to your body.** Somewhere amidst the turmoil, I understood that this experience was not just a moment of weakness; it was my body sending a distinct message. It wanted rest, healing, and understanding. This was not the first time I felt this way. In fact, I had come to recognize a pattern—a flare-up often followed the end of a stressful time or the exertion of energy I hadn't anticipated. It was my body's way of saying, "Enough. We need time to recoup."

The truth was harsh and undeniable. It wasn't just that I'd simply worn myself down; it was the constant battle I had been waging against my own limitations while trying to meet the unwritten expectations of a society that glorifies busyness and productivity. In my quest to keep up, I had attached my self-worth to my output, and now, lying in bed, unable to even lift my legs, I felt as though I had lost a crucial piece of myself.

"This is the new norm," I reminded myself despondently, as I tried to reconcile the woman I once was—the go-getter who thrived on little sleep, caffeine, and an endless drive—and the reality of the fatigued woman who needed rest not just now, but often. Underlying that acceptance was a deeper truth: the harsh realization that the fatigue I felt extended far beyond the physical; it seeped into my gut, wrapped around my self-esteem, and whispered ugly lies about my worthiness. I felt like an imposter in my own life—too weak, too lazy to get up and face the world.

A new understanding began to form. The silence of my immobility—even amidst the chaos of my thoughts—provided a space for reflection. There was a message nestled within the conflict, one that gently urged me to listen to my body, to honor its natural rhythms. I'd been pushing against those rhythms for far too long, battling against what felt like weakness, when in fact, it was a profound act of courage to simply stop.

Days like this became frequent—each one arriving after periods of intense stress, travel, or overstimulation. Each episode was a reminder that while my mind was willing to power through, my body had its limits, and it was finally voicing its demands. Recognizing this pattern became pivotal in my journey toward healing. I started to see each refusal of my body to comply as an invitation—a call to rest and recalibrate. Rather than fight against it, I began to lean into it.

In the past, I fought against these moments. The voices in my head echoed harshly: "You're weak. You're lazy. You have so much to do." This mental battle whipped me into a frenzy, focusing on all the things I wasn't accomplishing during these bouts of immobility. Instead of offering myself compassion during these hard times, I chose self-criticism—a destructive and exhausting practice.

But that day, lying helplessly in the confines of my bed, I began to grasp that it was okay to not be okay. The journey was steeped in layers of frustration, anger, disappointment, and fear. It became glaringly clear that this was going to be my new norm, at least for now.

I had hoped that by ignoring my body's needs, I would force it to comply with my relentless pace. However, the reality was that my body was in charge, and it had no intention of letting me speed through life without consequences. That morning was a sobering reminder of my limitations.

How could I find the strength to move through this?

I sat with my thoughts—contemplating the journey ahead. I began to envision how I could transform this experience from a moment of despair to an opportunity for growth. After many days spent in reflection and therapy, seeking to understand this new chapter of my life, I recognized that acknowledging my limitations could open the door to self-compassion. I could learn to respect the signals from my body and plan accordingly.

As I reflected on these moments of deep exhaustion, I found myself diminishing the noise in my head. The perpetration of negative self-talk was relentless: "You're weak; you're lazy; look at all you're missing." But I had learned that fighting against my own body merely dug me deeper into shame and despair. When I reframed my understanding—embracing these days as signals from my body rather than failures—I slowly began to cultivate self-compassion.

Redefining Strength

Embracing my new reality didn't mean giving up hope; rather, it meant shifting how I defined my strengths. Identifying triggers became vitally important. I learned to anticipate moments of potential burnout and plan my life around them. For instance, long travels—something I'd previously embraced with reckless abandon—were now double and triple-checked in terms of how I scheduled my upcoming days. I recognized that weekends filled with energy-draining activities often required significant recovery time.

The act of scheduling rest became pivotal. I intentionally carved out recovery time after any taxing engagements, routinely allowing my body the space it needed to heal and recuperate. My new normal included gentle boundaries—not just for myself, but for others as well. It meant I learned to say no, to prioritize my wellbeing over external expectations. This decision, adorned with trepidation and guilt, birthed a profound transformation. I stopped bursting from fatigue after my work; instead, I leaned into the moments of stillness with grace, recognizing them as indicators of my humanity.

Like a gardener nurturing delicate seeds, I began to cultivate a deeper understanding of my capabilities, allowing myself the grace to rest and recharge. For instance, I made it a point to schedule lighter workloads for the days immediately following strenuous events. I learned to diversify my plans;

when I traveled, I made sure to set aside time afterward to recuperate without codependent guilt nagging at my conscience.

As I began safeguarding my energy like the precious resource it was, I transformed my understanding of productivity. I discovered that if I took the necessary time to recover, I could still accomplish remarkable things. My endurance races taught me to embrace a slower pace—a different kind of success. Although I might not be the fastest runner on the trail, each step I took resonated with the strength of resilience.

There was one instance during a time of emotional drought when I had registered for an endurance race—my body, however, was far from race-ready. With a gentle nudge from my inner voice, I tuned into my physical capacity and recognized that I could participate, but on my own terms. I embraced the slower pace; I learned to celebrate every stride; every moment spent consciously moving. In doing so, I'd found a piece of joy in my new normal, a reaffirmation that I could still compete but differently, and that my worth was not dictated by speed or performance.

I learned that fatigue is not a joke; it was a formidable opponent, and my expectations needed to be set anew. Tasks that once took mere minutes now stretched into hours, requiring patience and redefined metrics of success. I couldn't always push my body to fulfill every task, and learning to accept this was transformational.

Lessons From Stillness

One morning, weeks later, I awoke again in a haze of fatigue, but this time the emotional landscape I traversed was different. I had committed to listening rather than challenging my body's messages. I would let the heavy morning rest on my shoulders without rushing to lift it off. On that specific day, I propped myself up with pillows, reached for a journal, and just began to write instead of fight. It was a practice born from the need to document my journey, to unravel the chaos swirling within and transform it into moments of clarity.

Each day was a small victory. I started mapping my triggers and how they interplayed with my energy levels—my travel fatigue, the intensity of public speaking engagements, and even interactions that depleted me when I was already running low. I knew weekends would leave me dragging into Mondays, and long days of work or travel would have implications for the following week. At first, it felt like a heavy burden to regulate my life so scrupulously, but the more I leaned into this self-awareness, the more empowered I began to feel.

This slow-down didn't just change my physical abilities; it morphed my internal dialog entirely. Instead of seeing it as a failure, I started to view my moments of rest as acts of bravery. I had the courage to say no when life's demands threatened to overwhelm me, allowing compassion to spill over into the way I treated others. If I craved understanding, it would only be fair to extend that same kindness to myself. It was a powerful revelation—one that redefined my approach to life.

With each day, filled with quiet moments, I discovered the lessons taught by stillness. When I surrendered control over life's demands, I began to find nuggets of gratitude hiding within pain. The sunshine on my face during moments of reflection became a reminder that stillness could also be healing.

Connection Through Vulnerability

Even with this newfound insight, each day was a journey riddled with self-discovery underpinned by vulnerability and compassion. How often do we, as strong women, pride ourselves on resilience without fully acknowledging what we endure? How often do we wear anxiety and demands like armor, only to feel them weigh us down when no one is watching? I learned through this vulnerability that it takes incredible courage to admit we are struggling, to own our feelings, and to ask for help.

It was this openness, this authenticity to myself, that began to resonate beyond my private struggles.

By sharing my journey, I realized how many women were silently caught in similar storms, navigating their own battles while putting on the brave face expected of them. I started to witness the transformative power of community, how shared experiences can foster deep connections and understanding. We can become more than isolated warriors; we can form sisterhoods of support, lifting each other through our lowest moments

In sharing my struggles, something remarkable began to unfold. While I worried about how others would perceive my limitations, the truth was that honesty brought people closer. By being open about my experiences, I invited others into a deeper connection. I found strength in vulnerability; in sharing that I was not always okay, I allowed the beauty of connection to flourish through our shared humanity.

How liberating it became to talk honestly about what I faced. I let others know that while I may appear okay on the outside, internally, I was engaged in a daily struggle. Those connections turned into a sanctuary of understanding. I learned that people often sympathized and offered their compassion, forging bonds that helped me through the toughest moments.

Shifting The Narrative

The turning point arrived one afternoon while sitting by the window, watching the world go by. I began reflecting on the past months—a tapestry woven with trials, tears, and tenacity. Yet amidst the weight of my struggles, I felt an overwhelming sense of hope. I realized that vulnerability is an honest reflection that carries profound healing power. **Even the strongest people break. But breakdowns don't disqualify us—they refine us.**

This experience illustrated the heart of my journey: Surrendering to my limitations allowed me to cultivate gratitude for the abilities I still possessed. Instead of viewing my fatigue as an enemy, I embraced it as a friend that taught me to slow down, breathe, and simply be. The exhaustion I once fought against became a powerful teacher, instilling in me the lessons of patience and empathy for myself.

Each time I felt immobilized, I chose to view those moments as invitations rather than defeats. What I learned was that vulnerability could be my strength. It set the stage for authentic connection, creating a mirror through which I witnessed the struggles of others and ultimately realized that even the strongest of us can break without losing our essence. Life's storms can force us to stop, to reconsider, and to craft a new narrative—all while holding space for our shortcomings. For every storm inside, there's an opportunity for personal growth and revelation.

I learned to trust the process of slowing down; it was not synonymous with failure but rather a vital step toward transformation. Through each moment of surrender came the unveiling of a greater purpose—there in my lowest points, I discovered a strength that refused to be extinguished.

I emerged stronger from the stillness. Each painful morning was not just a reminder of my fragility, but rather a doorway leading to the realization that one does not have to always be moving to be growing. That sometimes, the most powerful breakthroughs are birthed in silence and solitude.

I couldn't always see the silver lining amidst pain, but through the act of embracing my vulnerability, I discovered the ability to transform from within. I learned that asking for help and allowing others to support me did not denote weakness; rather, it signified an openness that invites communal healing. The journey of navigating personal storms may be fraught with challenges, but it showcases the profound beauty of resilience and the power of grace.

Cultivating Compassion

As I pen this chapter, I encourage you to look beyond your low moments; they don't disqualify your strength. They refine it. God walks with us through the chaos and confusion. He meets us in the silence, amidst the breakdowns, and demonstrates that there's beauty in our fragility. It is in these serene pauses that we find clarity, the kind that reshapes us into more compassionate, resilient versions of ourselves.

You do not have to be in motion to be growing. It's perfectly okay to pause, breathe, and simply exist. This chapter is an invitation to grant yourself permission—permission to admit when you're not okay, to shoulder the weight without feigning lightness, to embrace self-compassion as an essential part of your healing journey. Acknowledge that vulnerability is not weakness; it's your truth, and in your truth lies the power to evolve.

If those around me could extend compassion, then surely, I could start with myself. **For self-compassion and care are the seeds of true strength.** The lessons I've learned become a guiding light for others navigating their own storms. May they realize that they, too, are capable of embracing their vulnerabilities and finding strength in the stillness.

So, to every woman navigating her storm, know this: your breakdowns do not define who you are. They can be the very moments that ignite deep transformation—beckoning you into a richer, more profound space of healing and authenticity. Invite those moments, lean into them, and from that place of stillness, let God lift you up. The world awaits your emergence, your strength, born anew.

Today, I stand not just as a survivor of difficult mornings, but as a testament to all who face personal storms. I carry with me the knowledge that God meets us in the middle of our mess—not just in moments of strength and success, but also within our silence and sorrow. The tender space of vulnerability becomes the sacred ground for personal growth, laying the foundation for future strength.

At the end of it all, I want to leave you with this reminder: You don't have to move to grow; sometimes, it is in the stillness that true transformation begins. As I continue this journey, may you also find permission to be gentle with yourself, to pause, breathe, and embrace the grace you deserve. **For in the chaos, we find our truest selves—refined, restored, and ready to rise anew.**

TIME 2 REFLECT. TIME 2 S.H.I.N.E.

"Sometimes the bravest thing you can do is just keep showing up."—
Brené Brown

This isn't about what I've done—it's about what's possible when you choose to Spread Hope, Inspiration aNd Encouragement in your own life and the lives of others.

S – Spread Hope:

Think of a time when you hit a wall—physically, emotionally, or spiritually—and didn't know how you'd get through.
What (or who) reminded you that hope still existed, even in the stillness?
How might your story bring comfort to someone else in a similar valley?

H – Highlight Inspiration:

When you were at your lowest, who showed up for you in ways you didn't expect?
What did their presence—or God's—teach you about compassion and strength?
How can you now be that same safe space for others?

I – Invest in Myself:

In moments of burnout, rest isn't optional—it's essential.
What's one thing you can do this week to rest, refill, or reconnect with your soul?
Choose something that feels restorative, not just productive.

N – Name My Truth:

What am I afraid to admit about how I really feel right now?
Write it down without editing or judging yourself.
Honesty is where healing begins.

E – Embrace the Journey:

What have you learned about yourself in the quiet, heavy moments—the ones no one saw?
How did God meet you there, and what did He begin to show you about His strength in your weakness?
Celebrate the courage it took just to ***keep breathing.***

CHAPTER 7

INVISIBLE ILLNESS, VISIBLE STRENGTH

The clock struck midnight, and I sat in darkness, feeling as though I was the lone soldier in an unseen war. My body ached, and in that silence, I could almost hear the whispers of doubt—was I truly strong enough to advocate for myself amid a world that prioritized visible illnesses? Moments earlier, I had attempted to share my journey with friends only to be met with polite nods that felt like thin veils over ignorance. Frustrated yet resolute, I resolved to transform that moment of despair into a call to gather both knowledge and courage. It was time to take a pivotal step back and uncover the hidden power within my story, one that could illuminate the unseen realities faced by so many living with chronic conditions and braving their own storms in silence.

The Power of Knowledge

Understanding chronic illness begins with knowledge. For too long, conditions like Sjögren's and Alopecia have sat quietly in the shadows, often buried beneath more commonly recognized names like Lupus or Multiple Sclerosis (MS). It wasn't until I was diagnosed that the reality of Sjögren's entered my world—a realm filled with confusion, questions, and a deep longing for clarity. With Sjögren's, I learned that many people, including myself, had never heard of it until it struck close to home.

Alopecia presented a similar experience; before my own diagnosis, I was unaware of its existence. Discovering that there are various forms of this disorder, from alopecia areata to traction alopecia, felt like peeling back layers of an onion—each layer revealing more complexity and overwhelming information. Compounded by the reality that I was grappling with migraines and chronic fatigue, each new Instagram post, medical paper, and family dinner conversation slowly morphed into a stark reminder of how little awareness existed for many chronic conditions.

This realization often leaves you vacillating between confusion and the overwhelming urge to learn everything possible about your condition. These autoimmune disorders and chronic conditions can feel isolating, particularly when they are often invisible to others. Many people, me included, often embark on their advocacy journey without even knowing where to begin.

However, the journey to advocacy begins with learning.

Step 1: Educate Yourself

The foundation of advocacy is knowledge. You cannot effectively advocate for awareness and understanding until you arm yourself with complex information regarding your condition. Google, while often looked upon with skepticism, can be a valuable starting point. However, differentiating between reliable sources and misinformation is key. I've found that organizations like Johns Hopkins and the Cleveland Clinic provide credible, in-depth resources that can help illuminate your path. These sources are more than just data points; they hold insights that clarify how these conditions operate in our bodies.

The leading associations related to specific chronic illnesses such as the Sjögren's Foundation, the Lupus Foundation of America, and the National Alopecia Areata Foundation should serve as lifelines in your educational journey. These hubs provide up-to-date research and community connections to truly understand the nuance of each condition. Diving deep into these resources not only enhances your understanding but empowers you to share this knowledge with others.

When researching, don't shy away from the complexity of these conditions. With autoimmune diseases, there are different manifestations and types—just like how Alopecia has various forms, Sjögrens is systemic and can manifest itself in various forms. This complexity can be overwhelming, especially since many people may not recognize the breadth of these conditions. But it can also make your experience feel both unique and shared, as you delve deeper into the intricacies of your health. This growing understanding equips you with the tools to advocate, explaining to others that these diagnoses aren't merely labels—they encompass a daily struggle that impacts life in profound ways.

Step 2: Partner with Healthcare Providers

Once you've educated yourself, the next step on this advocacy journey is to establish a strong partnership with healthcare providers. This is crucial, especially for conditions that may not be well understood by all doctors. This part of the journey often requires patience; appointments can take months to arrange, especially for specialists familiar with lesser-known conditions. When you finally have your appointment, the choice of doctor must be guided by their willingness to partner with you.

A healthcare provider's approach matters significantly—are they open-minded and patient-centered, or do they lean strictly toward conventional medicine? Your ideal provider should take the time to know your full background and listen genuinely to your experiences and symptoms.

During your initial consultation, pay attention to how they interact with you. Do they review your medical records? Do they listen? Do they ask questions? Are they open to exploring various treatment options, or do they insist on a single course of action? A good provider should not only provide treatment but consider you as a whole person—considering your feelings, preferences, and lifestyle. It is crucial for them to explain treatment options and potential outcomes, allowing for open dialogue about what works best for you.

Be prepared for some trial and error as you navigate this partnership. With varying levels of awareness and commitment to understanding chronic illness, not all healthcare providers will resonate with your needs. You may need to encounter several healthcare practitioners before finding one who understands your needs. This process requires persistence, but an empathetic relationship with your healthcare provider can significantly improve your quality of life. Take your time to find the right fit—someone who listens and embraces your suggestions can make a world of difference.

To secure an effective partnership, ensure that the provider respects your input and is willing to explore various treatment modalities beyond just medication. This could mean utilizing a mix of conventional and alternative treatments to manage your illness holistically.

A collaborative relationship is built on trust, clarity, and a shared commitment to seeking the best possible outcome.

Step 3: Educate Your Family and Friends

Once you've built a network of support through trusted healthcare providers, it's time to bring your family into the conversation. The need for family education has proven to be one of the most challenging hurdles. When chronic conditions remain hidden in plain sight, it's often family—those who love us most—who struggle to comprehend the ongoing struggle.

Family members might need the most patience when it comes to framing your experiences in ways that resonate with them. Initially, my family struggled to grasp the severity of my conditions. Chronic illnesses often evoke skepticism, leading to misconceptions that you are exaggerating your symptoms—especially when your appearance does not reflect your inner turmoil.

Because these illnesses can be difficult to explain, your family might inadvertently dismiss your experiences. I recall expressing my frustrations about dealing with alopecia to my family members who were largely unaware of the effects of hair loss. The silence that followed felt louder than the audible gasps of misunderstanding. Nevertheless, it became crucial to approach these conversations with patience.

Begin by understanding how best to communicate with your family. What resonates with them? Some might appreciate articles that explain your condition, while others may be moved by personal stories or educational videos.

To help my family understand, I've employed various strategies tailored to individual personalities—some benefit from reading articles I provide, while others respond better to candid discussions. Start conversations, allowing family members to ask questions, and provide them with clear examples of how your illness affects your daily life. Don't shy away from sharing your story; personal testimonies and sharing your story can pave the way for deeper understanding and support. If your family struggles to comprehend your illness, share stories of others who face similar challenges. People often understand more when they see how others have been affected. It can take time for your family to grasp what you're experiencing, but relatable examples can help shorten that gap.

It is equally helpful to remember that sometimes, family members need to encounter these challenges personally before they can fully appreciate what chronic illness entails. This doesn't diminish your struggle; rather, it underlines the unfortunate truth of human empathy—the connection often deepens when the affliction is experienced directly.

Step 4: Create a Meaningful Support System

As the road continues, a strong support system becomes invaluable. Effective communication is crucial for ensuring your family understands your needs, but so is encouraging meaningful support. When dealing with chronic illnesses, it's vital to express what support looks like for you. For example, if stress exacerbates your condition, ask your family to help minimize stressful situations. A challenge emerges when the desired support from family doesn't materialize in the expected ways.

Over time, I have realized that support doesn't always come from the expected sources. For me, this meant turning to friends, peer groups, and community resources, including my church. Connecting with others who understand can create a safety net of emotional support. Seek out those who are empathetic, listen without judgment, and provide encouragement. It's vital to share your needs with those around you and establish what support looks like for you—be it emotional, physical, or even logistical.

It is essential to convey that support can take various forms. Whether it's simple check-ins, assistance with chores, or just an ear to listen can significantly reduce your burden and demonstrate that your loved ones acknowledge your fight.

In moments when stress exacerbates my condition, the burden becomes lighter when someone lends an ear or assists with everyday tasks. Advocacy extends beyond awareness; it thrives within a circle of people who recognize your journey and seek to approach your struggles with compassion and understanding.

Step 5: Broaden the Circle of Awareness

Once you've established understanding with your inner circle, the next stage is to broaden the advocacy to a wider audience. Your awareness-raising efforts can extend into the world beyond. This might include local groups, community organizations, or even social media platforms. Being open about your journey is a powerful tool for advocacy. Many women with chronic illnesses find themselves grappling with a tendency to downplay their experiences to avoid appearing overly dramatic. Sharing your story publicly can shine light on the invisible battles many face. The battle between asserting one's reality and fearing judgment creates an internal tension that can feel isolating. Advocating at a broader level necessitates recognizing the fine line between sharing information and inundating your audience with negativity. It requires a delicate balance, as you don't want to come across as complainant yet feel the need to highlight the real and often painful aspects of daily life with chronic illness.

As you step into broader circles—whether on social media, in professional settings, or other social engagements—deliberate on how to present your story authentically.

Begin by focusing on educating those around you in a way that fosters understanding without overshadowing your resilience. Share personal triumphs—no matter how small—celebrating the victories reminds both you and your audience that strength manifests in quiet, yet relentless determination.

When you share your journey, try to maintain a positive yet realistic approach. This doesn't diminish the struggle but instead allows those outside your circle to engage with your narrative. Consider adopting a storytelling approach—sharing highlights of your battles, triumphs, and everything in between. Sharing insights brings awareness, and when people gain insight, they're often more compassionate in their interactions with you and others who face similar challenges.

Social media can amplify your voice, especially by sharing credible resources and stories from other advocates. On social media, I consciously choose to frame my advocacy in ways that educate without overwhelming. Sharing credible articles, success stories, and research findings opens discourse without coming across as self-indulgent. Championing other people's experiences can often resonate more significantly than recounting your struggles; when public figures share their battles with similar chronic illnesses, the ripple effects are powerful.

Consider joining social media platforms where you can share experiences without fear of judgment. Sharing educational articles from credible sources can elevate discussions beyond your personal narratives, inviting others to find and share their stories.

In this ongoing effort to raise awareness, never underestimate the power of shared stories. They reveal that daily battles are not sung about in headlines or mainstream media, yet they are fought courageously in homes worldwide. Eventually, it helps not only the chronic sufferer but also the larger community of individuals who feel isolated in their experiences.

Step 6: Focus on Mental and Emotional Well-Being

Throughout this journey, I've learned about the importance of balance. As chronic illness advocates, we walk a narrow path where we must celebrate small victories while being candid about our struggles. It's tempting to gloss over the intricacies of chronic pain to appear capable and "normal"; however, striving for authenticity is essential.

Part of navigating chronic illness is addressing the emotional burden it can create. Recognize and articulate the mental toll that experience takes, and share this with others. The pressures of appearing "normal" despite internal struggles can be both exhausting and isolating. Finding the right balance between honesty and overshare is crucial. People often forget that the “visible” aspects of life may not reflect the internal battles. It’s essential to navigate mental and emotional health when chronic pain weighs heavy on your spirit. Each time I feel overwhelmed, I remind myself that asking for support is a strength and not a weakness.

Using social media as a platform can be particularly effective here, as it opens a space for discussion and solidarity on mental health matters. You may hesitate to share everything you cope with, but cultivating a community where open discussions about mental health exist empowers not just you, but others who are silently struggling elsewhere.

Every story shared adds to a growing narrative that chronic illnesses, while often invisible, bring recognizable challenges to the table. By pulling back the curtain on mental health's impact, you help show that strength does not reside solely in visible victories.

Strength in Vulnerability

As we venture through the challenges presented by invisible illnesses, remember that your strength does not always wear a cape. It doesn’t need to wave banners of success for others to see; it may be a soft whisper in the face of adversity, or the quiet perseverance to face each day with courage. Strength doesn’t always look like what the world expects. Remind people that while strength is often measured in visible successes, true resilience can be as subtle as enduring pain while still getting out of bed each day. Strength, in your narrative, is not loud. It’s in the small victories—the days you rise despite fatigue, the moments you share your truth, the times you seek help when needed. By pulling back the curtain on your journey, you create a space for understanding and support, even when things feel tough.

Chronic illness may be invisible, but the courage it demands is undeniable. The battles we face are life-altering and complex, intensifying our capacity for resilience. We're tasked with the daunting prospect of educating others while advocating for our needs. Our mission extends beyond raising awareness solely for ourselves; it involves heralding compassion over assumptions. It is about providing a voice for those who can't advocate for themselves and celebrating unseen victories that, although small, are monumental. By leading with compassion rather than assumptions, you encourage understanding that invisible illnesses are just as real and life-altering as those that can be seen.

This chapter unveils a truth—what we often see on the surface is merely the tip of the iceberg.

Embrace the Journey

In this journey, may we challenge ourselves and others to empathize, advocate, and celebrate every arduous step along our paths. Through understanding and resilience, we are sculpting a culture of compassion, one voice at a time.

Your advocacy can inspire others to recognize the unseen battles fought by many individuals living with chronic illnesses.

Celebrate your journey, embrace your strengths, and acknowledge the small victories, even when they remain hidden from the outside world. As you do, you reaffirm that it is not the visible battles we encounter that define our worth, but rather the quiet, consistent strength we muster in our greatest trials.

Perhaps the most crucial aspect of this journey is the acceptance that chronic illness does not define you. These conditions may be a part of your life, but they do not encapsulate your identity. You are more than your struggles; you are a tapestry woven from experiences that amplify your strength and resilience.

Strength does not always fit into the world's expectation; it often appears as mere survival on difficult days. Chronic illnesses may remain invisible to others, but the fortitude required to face each day diminishes no one's spirit. The battles fought daily may go unseen, yet they are undeniably real.

Fostering this awareness is not merely an act of advocacy; it's a call to empathy. Chronic illness may not always appear visible, but it yields an undeniable strength for those navigating its complex terrain. In wielding your story as a tool for understanding and compassion, you forge a path for others to reclaim their strength and purpose amidst the storms of life.

TIME 2 REFLECT. TIME 2 S.H.I.N.E.

"You never know how strong you are until being strong is your only choice." — Bob Marley

This isn't about what I've done—it's about what's possible when you choose to Spread Hope, Inspiration aNd Encouragement in your own life and the lives of others.

S – Spread Hope:

Chronic illness can feel like a hidden battle.
Who in your life (or in your own story) needs to hear that they're not alone—that their quiet struggle still matters?
What can you say or do to help them feel seen and heard?

H – Highlight Inspiration:

Who has inspired you by how they handle chronic illness, pain, or challenges you can't fully understand?
What about their journey resonates with you—and how can you honor that example in your own life?

I – Invest in Myself:

Living with or supporting someone with an invisible illness can be draining.
What's one thing you can do to refill your emotional and spiritual cup this week?
It could be as simple as a quiet moment of prayer, a walk outside, or a creative hobby.

N – Name My Truth:

What's one truth you want to acknowledge today about your health, your limits, or your needs?
Write it down and speak it out. Owning your truth isn't weakness—it's freedom.

E – Embrace the Journey:

How can you honor both the hard parts of this journey and the small victories?
What would it look like to show yourself (or someone you love) grace, even when progress feels slow?
Remember: every day you keep going is a win.

CHAPTER 8

HEALING IS MORE THAN A DIAGNOSIS

As the storm raged outside, I sat curled up on my couch, a cup of herbal tea in hand, frantically flipping through pages of holistic wellness books. My life had spiraled into chaos—an autoimmune disorder had turned my body against me, leaving me exhausted and adrift in a sea of uncertainty. But beneath the thunder and rain, a small flicker of hope ignited within me. Little did I know, this storm would lead me to discover the interconnectedness of my body, mind, and spirit—what true healing really meant.

The Roots of Holistic Wellness

Holistic wellness is an expansive concept, one that encompasses more than just physical health—it integrates the emotional, mental, and spiritual aspects of one's being. To me, holistic wellness represents the intricate interplay between these dimensions, ensuring that every part of ourselves is nourished and functioning harmoniously. Throughout my journey, I've come to realize that healing is not merely a response to illness; it's an ongoing commitment to nurturing the whole self, body, mind, spirit, and soul.

In college, I pursued a pre-med biology degree with aspirations of entering medical school, largely drawn to the scientific side of healing. However, as time progressed, my interest gravitated toward osteopathic medicine—an approach that seeks to address the root causes of health issues rather than merely alleviating symptoms. This realization shifted my perspective entirely. It was no longer just about treating conditions but about comprehensively understanding the individual and the complexities of their health.

This newfound curiosity deepened during my travels throughout Asia. Immersed in Eastern practices and philosophies, I discovered that healing could be approached through diverse modalities. Here, I began to appreciate the power of touch during my time studying massage therapy, especially reflexology. Each stroke, each gentle knead of the muscle, carried an energy that resonated far beyond the physical realm. The fact that a certain spot on your foot corresponded to a different body part, and the state of that body part could be deciphered from pressing on the feet was mind-blowing to me. Bodies are vessels of experience, and how we treat them can profoundly affect our wellness.

In the military, my experiences as a resilience instructor introduced me to the concept of holistic well-being through the "pillars" of wellness: emotional, physical, spiritual, and mental. These pillars reinforced the idea that true strength comes from nurturing every facet of our existence. I had once thought that to be strong, one must merely push through barriers instead of acknowledging when one needs to pause, rest, and reflect.

The Power of Nutrition

A pivotal moment on this journey unfolded in 2008—one that would change my approach to nourishment forever. It all began at a Sam's Club when I stumbled upon a Vitamix demonstration. "You can invest now or pay later," the demonstrator said. His assertion struck me deeply. Investing in a high-quality blender meant enabling a lifestyle where nutritious, whole foods would become the norm rather than an exception. It underscored the importance of making conscious choices—not just for immediate gratification but for long-term health. The decision to divert from processed foods to embracing vibrant fruits and vegetables was transformative. Nutrition became not a mere dietary adjustment but a foundational principle of my holistic wellness practice.

Nutrition is the backbone of holistic wellness; it's the canvas upon which one paints their daily life. Acknowledging the healing properties found in nature—those antioxidants nestled within berries, the vitamins in leafy greens—helped me embrace a higher quality of life. As I delved deeper, my understanding of the toxins in everyday products struck a chord. It became evident that many illnesses faced today are exacerbated by environmental factors, a reality that pushed me toward embracing more natural, plant-based, and whole food diets.

Rest as a Healing Tool

Living in other countries revealed striking contrasts to American lifestyles. I noticed that communities abroad prioritize family time and rest; the concept of "work-life balance" holds substantial significance. Their cultural practices promote wellness organically, seamlessly threading nutrition, activity, and rest into the fabric of daily life. Adopting these principles greatly enriched my holistic wellness journey.

Mindfulness has been an integral aspect of my growth. I learned that the narratives we tell ourselves—our inner dialogues—shape our experiences and influence our emotional states. It's simpler to lead a happy life with positive thoughts than to dwell in negativity. Embracing mindfulness practices has transformed not just how I respond to challenges, but how I cultivate joy in each moment, revealing the intricate connections between thought and well-being.

Resting for replenishment became a lesson I learned through necessity. Living with an autoimmune disorder forced me to confront a reality that many ignore: the body requires time to recover and regenerate. I once thought rest was a sign of weakness; now, I understand it as an essential component of wellness. With each restorative night, I became in tune with my body's signals. I've realized that it's not about the number of hours but about quality; true rest distinguishes itself with clarity and energy that carries into the next day.

At the heart of my holistic approach lies a profound faith, which serves as my anchor during life's turbulent times. My faith—rooted deeply in my relationship with Jesus Christ—provides both strength and purpose. It lifts me during my darkest hours and fuels my passion for life. Understanding that everything happens for a reason, and recognizing that my journey is intentional has empowered me to work with a mindset of gratitude and grace. This foundation has inspired me to explore my purpose and embrace the calling I have; to foster wellness in others.

Community has played an undeniable role in propelling me towards holistic wellness. My encounter with a company that focused on botanical products ignited my passion for healthier alternatives. I immersed myself in acquiring knowledge about essential oils, clean beauty products, and natural remedies. This newfound community surrounded me with like-minded individuals whose ardor for wellness became contagious, affecting not only my choices but my perspective. These connections threw open doors to realms of functional medicine and holistic health coaching, allowing me to expand my knowledge further and actively contribute to the wellness of those around me.

The Interconnectedness of Well-Being

If you're ready to embark on your journey towards holistic wellness, my advice is simple yet profound: take control of your health and recognize that it's interconnected. Your emotions influence your thoughts, and these thoughts dictate your choices. Honor your emotions; embrace each aspect of yourself as interconnected and vital to your well-being. Integrate healthy practices in all areas of your life and be intentional. Create a nourishing environment—both physically and emotionally. Engage with whole foods and become conscious stewards of what you consume, both in eating and in the products you use. Surround yourself with people who amplify your wellness journey, lifting you during challenging times and celebrating your victories.

As you dissect the many components of wellness—nutrition, mindset, rest, faith, and joy—you'll discover that they are not merely separate strands but part of a larger tapestry of healing. Understanding this integral relationship will foster a gratitude for every facet of your journey. Healing transcends the temporal act of treating ailments; it manifests in an empowered daily practice of nurturing every dimension of ourselves.

Joy in the Everyday

True healing isn't merely about managing symptoms; it is about cultivating a life that honors and nurtures your wholeness and purpose. As you explore these dimensions of wellness, recognize that joy, rest, and faith are as vital as nutrition and movement. Actively seek joy in the small, sacred moments—even amidst struggles. Give yourself permission to honor your limits without apology and prioritize rest without guilt.

This chapter can be a turning point, an invitation to design a holistic life that embodies the entirety of your being. Remember, you are worth every investment it takes to embark on this journey. Let this journey be one of rediscovery—of leaning into your strengths while embracing your vulnerabilities. You are not alone; many women navigate similar storms, each carrying their story, waiting to intertwine with others in a beautiful, shared tapestry of resilience and healing.

As we redefine what healing entails, may we recognize that it's not a destination but an ongoing endeavor. Each choice we make contributes to a rich, fulfilling life worth celebrating—a life where healing flourishes beyond diagnosis and illuminates a path towards harmony and wholeness.

TIME 2 REFLECT. TIME 2 S.H.I.N.E.

"Healing doesn't mean the damage never existed. It means the damage no longer controls your life."— Akshay Dubey

This isn't about what I've done—it's about what's possible when you choose to Spread Hope, Inspiration aNd Encouragement in your own life and the lives of others.

S – Spread Hope:

Think about someone in your life who needs to hear that healing is more than just what's happening in their body.
How can you be a voice of hope for them, reminding them they're more than their diagnosis?

H – Highlight Inspiration:

Who has modeled true, holistic wellness for you—someone who shows how faith, joy, and mindset make a difference?
What can you learn from their journey?

I – Invest in Myself:

What's one small step you can take today to care for your whole self—body, mind, and spirit?
It could be a nourishing meal, a walk in nature, a prayer, or simply pausing to breathe deeply.

N – Name My Truth:

What truth about your health or self-care journey have you been avoiding? Write it down. Acknowledge that you're worth the effort it takes to heal in every area of your life.

E – Embrace the Journey:

What does giving yourself grace look like right now?
How can you celebrate the progress you've made in caring for your whole self, even if it doesn't look perfect?

CHAPTER 9

PURPOSE OVER PERFECTION

The argument reached its peak, leaving both me and my daughter in tears—two flawed individuals caught in the middle of a personal storm. I paused for a moment, feeling completely overwhelmed by the pressure to be the 'perfect' parent. It was then that I realized that chasing perfection was not just tiring; it was suffocating. This chapter of my life was calling for change, inviting me to trade in the need for flawlessness for something far richer: a journey filled with purpose.

Embracing Imperfection

In the tumultuous landscape of motherhood, I've learned that embracing imperfection is not just an option; it's a necessity for survival. My journey towards embracing imperfection has been one filled with twists, turns, and an abundance of lessons that I continue to navigate today. As a single mother of two daughters from different fathers—neither of whom play an active part in their lives—my experiences are deeply etched in the fabric of my daily routine and struggles. It's easy to think of imperfection as a heavy weight, pulling us under, but it can also be a source of growth, understanding, and, ultimately, a more fulfilling life.

Perfection, which many strive for in various areas of their lives, is an illusion. It's like chasing a mirage; it shimmers in the distance but never truly gets closer. Instead, we must challenge ourselves to find purpose in our lives, accepting that it's okay to be flawed. Over the years, I have realized that what matters most isn't the picture-perfect image I might want to project but the authenticity and purpose I choose to embody.

Life has a way of presenting us with challenges that force our hand. It demands that we confront our fears of inadequacy, especially when faced with expectations—both internal and external—that are often unattainable. Navigating the complexities of raising two daughters with different needs and backgrounds, I learned this lesson the hard way. I could easily compile a long list of my perceived failures: a military career cut short, less-than-stellar relationships, and the daunting task of parenting during turbulent teenage years. Each of these listings could fill a volume on imperfection, but rather than focusing solely on what's wrong, I choose to view these moments through the lens of growth.

Power of Connection

Transitioning into motherhood for the second time has shown me the beauty of letting go of societal expectations. Rather than striving to be that mythical "supermom"—a figure often glorified but rarely attainable—I've learned to focus on what truly matters: my connection with my daughter and the experiences we share. I learned to approach parenting by listening to her needs, attempting to understand her outbursts as expressions of her struggles rather than signs of my failures. This shift in perspective has changed everything for our relationship.

Once I released myself from worrying about the opinions of others—about how rocking the "imperfect" boat might ruffle some feathers—I opened the space for genuine moments of connection with my daughter. Instead of reacting with frustration to her outbursts, I leaned in to understand her world, a world filled with confusion and raw emotion. I learned that many of her actions were cries for help—a plea to be seen and heard in a chaotic landscape of adolescence.

Finding Your Own Purpose

Each week, I strive to embody what it means to place purpose over perfection. One evening, as I sat on my daughter's bed, listening to her share the details of her day, I witnessed the beauty of vulnerability unfold. She wasn't asking for solutions; she was sharing her heart, her fears, her struggles. In that moment, I realized my purpose wasn't to get everything right or enforce discipline but to walk alongside her in her journey—flawed and all.

So how do we focus on purpose over perfection? The first step is simple yet profound: control what you can. Accept that some things are beyond your influence. This concept was grounding for me: why spend time worrying about things that I cannot change? Instead, I remind myself that I can take steps forward with the resources I do have. If I acknowledge where my gaps are, I can either find ways to fill them or learn to work around them.

This realization sparked the idea that I don't need to be flawless to achieve my purpose. This doesn't mean I shouldn't strive for excellence or improvement; rather, it's about learning to be at peace with where I am. Just thinking about the phrase, "If God gives you a vision, He will provide," helps me transition from fear of inadequacy to understanding that I am supported in my journey.

In the military, we often used a phrase about striving for excellence while being satisfied with what we could achieve. This doesn't mean lowering our standards; rather, it's about acknowledging our finite capabilities and moving forward strategically. When I recognize that I possess an unwavering calling—

a purpose rooted in love and service—I find that my perceived shortcomings become secondary to the mission at hand.

A good starting point for many might be conducting a simple SWOT analysis. List your Strengths and Weaknesses, then identify Opportunities and Threats in your life. This strategy helps clarify where you can invest your energy. Each small victory along the way—be it learning a new skill or reaching out for support—validates the progress I make, which brings us to our next step: taking action.

For me, purpose isn't just the "what" but also the "why" behind my actions. If I can stay anchored in that purpose, the cracks in my armor—those moments where I fall short—don't define me. Rather, they enhance my authenticity. The journey becomes richer, more meaningful, and certainly more relatable.

Redefining Success

Perhaps you, dear reader, struggle with feelings of inadequacy stemming from the unrealistic expectations society thrusts upon us. Here's the thing: perfection is an illusion that only serves to imprison us in a cycle of self-doubt and anxiety. When we measure our lives against others—whether it's a polished Instagram post or a neighbor's seemingly perfect family—we lose sight of our unique journeys. It's essential to redefine what success looks like for you.

By embracing imperfection, I've transformed my outlook on success. I remember attending a leadership conference where speakers echoed a powerful mantra: "If you keep waiting to get it right, you'll always be waiting." They urged us to take action, to learn as we went. It felt liberating to consider that success does not lie in flawlessness but in moving forward despite shortcomings.

In reflecting on my time in the military, the term "flawless execution" was thrown around often in performance reviews. It created a culture of pressure, where any mistake felt monumental. But I soon learned that striving for excellence rather than perfection is far more meaningful. It reminds us that mistakes are part of learning, part of growth.

I encourage everyone, especially women navigating their own storms, to redefine success beyond the flawless facade. Life isn't perfectly packaged, and pursuing purpose enables us to embrace the unpredictable nature of our journeys. So often, we're told to chase after the ideal; a perfect plan, a perfect look, a perfect score. But what happens when we fall short? We are left feeling inadequate.

Consider this—the more we link our self-worth to perfection, the more it erodes our joy. Life becomes a constant struggle of comparing ourselves to an unrealistic standard. I used to think that being flawless defined success. However, the truth is that embracing my imperfections has led to greater satisfaction in life. When I decided to be satisfied with doing something well, rather than worrying about flawless execution, my life transformed.

Living with grace instead of hustle doesn't mean you abandon your ambitions or purposes. It means that you approach your goals with compassion rather than criticism. When I think about the things I want to achieve, I remind myself: it's okay if I stumble along the way; what matters is that I keep moving. Embracing imperfection allows room for growth. It frees us from the need to perform for others and instead propels us toward a life centered on our core values and beliefs.

Celebrate Progress

It's crucial to cultivate a mindset that celebrates progress over perfection. Remember those moments when you felt overwhelmed by the pressure to excel? It's easy for all of us to feel like failures when we slip up. Yet, those slips can teach us. Allowing ourselves to be vulnerable offers genuine connection and understanding not just with others, but with ourselves.

Practical Steps to Progress

Now, some practical steps can aid in this journey:

1. **Control What You Can:** Identify areas in your life that are within your control, and focus your energy there. If something is outside that realm, acknowledge it and release it. This shift eases the pressure we often place on ourselves unnecessarily.

2. **Reflect on Your Purpose:** Clarify your core values. Write down your goals and ask yourself, "Are these rooted in my truth, or are they shaped by external expectations?" Make adjustments as needed to align your actions with your purpose.

3. **Adopt a Growth Mindset:** Embrace the notion that failures are simply lessons in disguise. When you shift from a fixed mindset—which views mistakes as setbacks—to a growth mindset, you transform challenges into opportunities.

4. **Practice Vulnerability:** Share your journey with trusted friends, family, or community members. Opening up about challenges helps dissolve the illusion of perfection. When you express your struggles, you not only lighten your burden but also forge deeper connections with others.

5. **Celebrate Small Wins:** Instead of focusing solely on ultimate achievements, take time to acknowledge small milestones along the way. Each step forward, no matter how minor, is a testament to your perseverance and growth.

6. **Be Satisfied with Excellence:** Strive for excellence but recognize that there's beauty in imperfections. The perfect mother doesn't exist; rather, the successful one is the one who shows up, learns, and loves authentically.

Authentically Human

In our hyper-connected world, we often showcase our highlights and curate our brands, but this façade can strip away authenticity. The more polished we appear, the less real we feel. Embracing your flaws makes you relatable; it reminds you and others that being human isn't about what you do flawlessly but rather about how authentically you show up.

Letting go of the need to impress frees you to embrace your authenticity and gives you permission to be fully human—flawed but fierce, imperfect but purposeful. Your unique journey matters. The world doesn't need more perfect people; it needs more genuine ones. So release the pressure to perform or prove yourself. Embrace the messy, beautiful journey of growth—even if it's not Instagram-perfect.

What will happen when you release the need to perform flawlessly? You free yourself to live boldly. The next time I feel that pressure building inside me, I'll pause. I'll remember the hard-won lessons that imperfection has taught me. Instead of succumbing to uncertainty, I'll step forward fueled by purpose. Creating and nurturing connections can be messy, but it's also rewarding beyond measure.

So, what if instead of focusing on the glittering ideal of perfection, we chose to appreciate the beauty of being human? Life is filled with ups and downs, joy and heartache. It's our experiences in the real world—not the Instagram-perfect moments—that craft who we are. When we embrace the messy, beautiful journey of growth, we allow ourselves to find contentment and courage while pursuing our greater purpose.

Breakthrough

For every woman out there who feels overwhelmed by the societal standards of perfection, remember this: life isn't about doing everything flawlessly. It's about living your purpose boldly and authentically. It's about showing up, taking action, learning along the way, and loving yourself and others through the struggles.

Ultimately, my message to you is this: are you ready to embrace your journey for what it really is? Each step of progress reminds us of how far we've come, celebrating the flawed, fierce individuals we truly are. Even as I write these words amid my imperfect life, I urge you to remember—you're allowed to be human. Acknowledge your flaws but let them fuel your journey towards something bigger. You're not just in life to chase perfection; you're here to thrive in all your beautiful, imperfect ways.

TIME 2 REFLECT. TIME 2 S.H.I.N.E.

"I am not what happened to me, I am what I choose to become."— Carl Jung

This isn't about what I've done—it's about what's possible when you choose to Spread Hope, Inspiration aNd Encouragement in your own life and the lives of others.

S – Spread Hope:

Who in your life needs to hear that they are enough, even in their imperfections?

What could you say to them today to help lift the weight of perfection off their shoulders?

H – Highlight Inspiration:

Think of someone you admire—not for what they've achieved, but for how they live with purpose and authenticity.
How does their example inspire you to let go of perfection in your own life?

I – Invest in Myself:

What's one way you can take the pressure off yourself this week?
Maybe it's giving yourself permission to rest, to play, or to say "no" to something that doesn't align with your purpose.

N – Name My Truth:

What's one truth about yourself or your journey that you've been afraid to admit because it doesn't look perfect?
Write it down and own it—imperfection is where growth and beauty live.

E – Embrace the Journey:

How can you celebrate the small wins and progress you've made, even if they're not "perfect"?
What would it look like to give yourself credit for showing up with purpose, no matter what?

CHAPTER 10

SHINE ANYWAY

In the midst of chaos, just when she thought all was lost, a flicker of light danced before her eyes. Torn between despair and hope, she felt the weight of the world on her shoulders, crushing her spirit. How could she possibly rise above the storm when every effort seemed futile? Yet, in that pivotal moment, something shifted within her—a whisper reminding her that even in the darkest nights, the stars still shone brightly. As the clouds began to dissipate, she took a deep breath and prepared to uncover the resilience that resided within, ready to inspire others to do the same.

The Birth of SHINE

When the clouds gather and the storms of life rage, it's tempting to succumb to despair, to feel lost amidst the turmoil. Yet, here is where the power of the philosophy "SHINE Anyway" comes into play. At its essence, the philosophy embodies a commitment to Spread Hope, Inspiration, and Encouragement regardless of the challenges that threaten to cloud our hearts and minds. It's a call to action, a beacon of light that reminds us, especially women navigating personal storms, that even in the darkest moments, we possess the ability to shine bright.

You see, life is full of storms—those tough moments when everything feels overwhelming. Maybe you're feeling sad or anxious, or perhaps you're dealing with a tough situation at work or with your family. Regardless of the circumstances, the philosophy of SHINE Anyway encourages us to rise above the chaos. It invites us to be the light for ourselves and others, no matter how dark the clouds in our lives may seem.

The genesis of this philosophy can be traced back to my startup journey back in 2021. As I sought to establish my brand, I turned to those around me, asking them what words defined my essence. The overwhelming feedback was simple yet profound: "inspiring," "encourager," and "hopeful." These words became the bedrock of my mission and transformed into the acronym SHINE. It serves as my daily reminder that life may not always be easy, but we are called to illuminate the paths of others, sharing warmth and positivity in a world rife with negativity.

SHINE with a smile

Everywhere we look—scrolling through social media or engaging in community discourse—we're confronted by cruelty and rampant negativity. The so-called "keyboard ninjas" unleash biting comments that chip away at our collective spirit. It's a painful reminder of how overwhelming the world can feel. This is why I am driven by a profound desire to counteract this tide of negativity, to be a force of kindness and positivity in an often harsh landscape. As I walk into a room, I hope to change the atmosphere, creating a space filled with hope and encouragement—a space where smiles can flourish, and hearts can uplift one another.

The smile is a powerful tool. It does not cost a thing but has the potential to change someone's day. When you walk into a room, do you want to bring a cloud of sadness, or do you want to lift the spirits of those around you? I've always believed in the power of a smile. My smile is one of my best assets, and I've found that it often opens doors for connection and kindness.

SHINE and Grow

In navigating my own challenges—some self-induced, others thrust upon me—I've come to appreciate the significance of resilience. While I may not have faced terminal illnesses or catastrophic losses, I have battled my share of shadows, navigating the scars left behind by unhealed childhood traumas. These experiences have not defined me; rather, they have shaped me into someone who recognizes the power of growth and learning. Every challenge presents an opportunity—an invitation to reflect and support others on their journeys.

The core lesson I want to impart is rooted in the tenet of perseverance: don't give up, believe in yourself, and, most importantly, learn to love yourself. Self-love is not a luxury; it's a necessity, and it lays the groundwork for all other relationships. Only when we nurture ourselves can we open our hearts to love others genuinely.

At the end of the day, our growth comes from these experiences. Your experiences aren't just for you; they are opportunities to help someone else. It's simply how life works. Sometimes, you may meet someone who needs your wisdom years later, at an unexpected time.

SHINE Through Words

Communication is key. Have you ever wondered WHY your co-worker, spouse, or child reacts a certain way in certain situations? What about that co-worker that ALWAYS needs attention? Or why your boss doesn't want a lot of details and gets frustrated with small talk? The day I learned the secret code to understanding human behavior, it changed everything! In the communication game, we must always see the individuals behind the behavior and be curious about the reasons for their actions. To communicate effectively—one of the essential skills in building meaningful relationships—I encourage others to seek out personality assessments, like DISC, which illuminated my understanding of my own behaviors and those of others. By learning to speak others' languages, we become adept at connecting with empathy rather than taking things personally, thus transforming our interactions and deepening our relationships.

SHINE with Gratitude

The journey to find one's own light amid life's storms begins with a realization: if you have breath in your body, you have the potential to shine. If you're feeling stuck or lost, first take a moment to acknowledge your feelings. Those emotions are real, and it's completely okay to feel that way. Think of those moments when life throws a storm your way. However, always remember there is light after the storm. Nature teaches us this—after heavy rain and grey skies, the sun shines once more, often resulting in rainbows. Your light comes from within you. It's your belief that gives it strength.

In recognizing the cyclical nature of storms and sunlight, we learn to embrace a mindset of gratitude. Gratitude isn't merely a feel-good emotion; it is a deliberate choice and a powerful tool in transforming our struggles into opportunities. When faced with daunting challenges, I've learned to shift my focus from what I lack to the abundance that exists around me. The small things—a smile from a stranger, a moment of peace, no traffic, catching all the green lights, or the simple act of being alive—become sources of immense joy and appreciation. This gratitude shifts perception; it reframes obstacles as avenues for growth and not as barriers to our success.

An example of this shift occurred during a particularly overwhelming phase in my life, where financial burdens felt like they were crashing down around me. In the grip of anxiety, I found it was all too easy to focus on my struggles—

emergency car repairs, unexpected bills that never seemed to cease. But reminding myself of the roof over my head, cool air from the brutal heat outside, the food in my pantry, and the clean running water along with two healthy and thriving daughters, gave me a renewed perspective. It was a powerful realization that despite my challenges, countless blessings existed in my life.

The world can be overwhelming, but when you embrace the thought of gratitude, everything changes. It requires effort and will not always be easy, but like any muscle, it will grow stronger with practice. Gratefulness isn't automatically granted to you; it's a choice. When life becomes challenging, retraining your brain to tap into gratitude can transform your focus.

As women navigating personal storms, we must remember that encountering difficulties isn't synonymous with defeat. With each challenge, you have a choice: you can allow the storms to drown your spirit, or you can rise, cherish your journey, and shine brightly for your own sake and for those who may benefit from your light. Remember that your experiences, your voice, and your journey matter deeply—even when they feel diminished by the struggles you face.

When feelings of being overwhelmed or lost creep in, I've found relief in engaging in activities that uplift my spirit and refocus my energy. Whether it's going for a run, dancing to my favorite music, or immersing myself in a creative endeavor, engaging in productive action can shatter the clouds of doubt. This is akin to the advice I'd share with my daughter when tackling daunting tasks: the way we perceive challenges often influences our outcomes. By choosing to cultivate positivity and embracing our journey, we radiate a light that can illuminate not only our path but also those around us.

SHINE in the Mind

The crucial link between mindset and daily practice in applying SHINE is simple but powerful: the connection between thought, word, and action. What we think influences what we say, which ultimately impacts what we do. Positive thoughts lead to encouraging words, driving positive actions. If you find yourself saying, "I'm tired," guess what? Your body will listen and respond accordingly.

Instead, whisper to yourself, "I am capable. I can tackle this challenge!" With practice, you'll find your outlook changing, your beliefs shifting, and your actions reflecting positivity. For a moment, let's visualize this together. Picture your mind as a garden. What seeds are you planting there? Are they seeds of negativity or seeds of hope? The ones you choose to nurture will indeed grow.

Everyday Actions to SHINE

Now, consider what SHINE-ing looks like in practical terms. You can cultivate your light daily by making simple choices:

- Start your day with gratitude.

When you wake up, think about one thing you're thankful for. Maybe it's a sunny morning or the warmth of your bed.

Then, as you go about your day,

- spread positivity to others.

Smile at someone, offer a kind word, or lend a helping hand.

These small actions can create ripples of light in the lives of those you encounter.

I hope these thoughts resonate with you: when you adopt the "I get to" perspective, it opens opportunities. Instead of seeing your challenges as burdens, begin viewing them as chances for growth. When I look at the obstacles in my life—a difficult situation, a difficult run, a hard day—I remind myself that I have the "get to" attitude. The choice lies with us.

Embrace Your SHINE

It's important to internalize that everyone possesses a unique light, a distinct narrative waiting to be told. While the world offers its share of challenges, the commitment to shine amid adversity stands as a testament to one's spirit. I recall countless stories of individuals who exemplified resilience—people enduring the unthinkable, like losing a child or fighting cancer, yet still choosing to inspire others. Their struggles didn't dim their spirit; instead, they became sources of strength, fueling their resolve to live passionately and share their light with others.

As you embark on this journey of self-discovery, I invite you to reflect on the ways you can reinforce your own SHINE philosophy. It begins with a mindset shift and a daily choice to pursue gratitude, positivity, and connection. Embrace your imperfections and recognize that they are part of your unique story; you are not meant to have it all together to impact lives. Your story matters—and it holds the potential to positively influence others who may find themselves lost in their own storms. Remember, you have everything needed to SHINE anyway. Don't wait until you feel perfect to step out and make a difference. Your voice matters, just as it is. When you embrace your imperfections as part of your story instead of hiding from them, you become more relatable and authentic.

Remember to SHINE

So, as you pave your path, I leave you with these essential reminders:

- Embrace yourself fully—your imperfections, your experiences—because the world needs your authenticity.

- Be brave enough to share your journey; you never know who needs to hear your story.

- Honor your struggles as they shape your growth, leading you toward a brighter tomorrow.

- Finally, commit to SHINE anyway, for the power of hope, inspiration, and encouragement radiates through you. You possess everything you need within you to navigate life's storms with grace and courage.

I encourage you to internalize this message: even amid darkness, you have the power to shine your light. Your presence matters; it's time to embrace your role as a beacon of hope and inspiration in the lives of others. There's beauty in resilience, and together, we can illuminate the world—one hopeful, encouraging act at a time. Shine anyway.

I want you to take with you the certainty that your light matters. Even in darkness, you can shine. Your journey may be full of twists and turns, but each step you take matters deeply. You were made for a purpose bigger than the storms you face. Your presence matters; it's time to embrace your role as a beacon of hope and inspiration in the lives of others. Embrace courage, purpose, and the creativity to live life fully. You don't need to have it all together to make a difference because your light is needed just as it is.

There's beauty in resilience and knowing you are more than your struggles. You have everything it takes to shine through every storm—so let your light shine. The world is waiting for you!

Together, we can illuminate the world—one hopeful, encouraging act at a time. SHINE anyway!

TIME 2 REFLECT. TIME 2 S.H.I.N.E.

"When you can't find the light, be the light."— Unknown

This isn't about what I've done—it's about what's possible when you choose to Spread Hope, Inspiration aNd Encouragement in your own life and the lives of others.

S – Spread Hope:

Who in your life could use a reminder today that their light matters—no matter what they're facing?
How can you encourage them to keep going and keep shining?

H – Highlight Inspiration:

What's one story—yours or someone else's—that shows the power of resilience and faith?
Reflect on how it challenges you to live boldly and share your light.

I – Invest in Myself:

What's one small thing you can do today to honor your light and purpose?
It could be speaking life over yourself, taking a bold step in faith, or simply resting in God's promises.

N – Name My Truth:

What fear or doubt is trying to dim your light?
Write it down and declare that you will shine anyway—because you're not defined by your struggles.

E – Embrace the Journey:

How can you remind yourself that your story is still unfolding, and your light is needed right now?
What would it look like to step into your purpose today, trusting that God will use your light for good?

EMBRACE YOUR RESILIENCE: CONCLUDING YOUR JOURNEY WITH "SHINE THROUGH THE STORM"

Congratulations, my people! As you close the final pages of *SHINE Through the Storm*, I want you to take a moment to acknowledge the courage it took to embark on this journey. You've equipped yourself with insights and practical strategies designed to help you weather personal storms, reclaim your strength, and reconnect with your purpose. The knowledge you've gained is not just information but a launching pad for transformative action in your life.

Throughout this book, I shared stories, strategies, and practices that resonate deeply, all with the aim of empowering women like you. Your experiences, your challenges, and your victories deserve to be shared, celebrated, and transformed into stories that encourage others. I urge you to speak up and share your experiences. When you voice your journey, you not only validate your own struggles but also provide a beacon of hope for fellow women who may feel lost in their storms.

Creating a safe space for yourself to journal your feelings is another vital takeaway. Look around you; the world is filled with noise, distractions, and pressures. Carve out a sanctuary – whether it's a cozy corner in your home or a quiet park – that allows you to reflect, process, and tap into your emotions. Writing can be a liberating experience. It's a chance for you to articulate your thoughts and feelings, turning your internal chaos into clarity. Trust me; your journal can become your best friend, offering comfort and insight as you navigate your path forward.

As you reflect on your journey so far, remember that forward movement is essential. Embrace the idea of progression rather than perfection. Incremental steps towards your goals can create monumental change over time. Whether it's deciding to learn a new skill, setting health goals, or advocating for your needs in relationships, take actionable steps that align with your vision of a fulfilled life. It's not always easy, but remember: true growth often occurs outside of our comfort zones.

Now, as you wrap up this chapter of *SHINE Through the Storm*, it's time to turn knowledge into action. I challenge you to create an actionable plan right now. Write down at least three specific actions you can take this week to advance toward your goals. Whether it's setting a coffee date with a mentor, enrolling in an online course, or simply starting to journal, make sure these actions are concrete.

These steps may seem small, but they are the foundation for overcoming obstacles that may stand in your way. Transitioning from thought to action is where real change happens. Remember: you are not alone in this journey. There is a community of women out there, each facing her own storms, ready to rise together.

So, what will it be? Will you let the storms keep you grounded, or will you rise above them and truly shine? The choice is yours, and I'm rooting for you every step of the way. Take a deep breath, let go of any remaining hesitations, and step boldly into the life you are meant to create. Your storm doesn't define you; your response to it does. Let's shine brightly, together!

UNYIELDING SPIRIT: TAMMY DOTSON'S JOURNEY FROM ADVERSITY TO EMPOWERMENT

Tammy Dotson wrote ***SHINE Through the Storm*** to inspire women from all walks of life who are navigating their own personal tempests. With a remarkable ability to turn challenges into triumphs, Tammy shares her journey of resilience, empowerment, and reclaiming strength and purpose. Through this book, she aims to provide a roadmap for women seeking to emerge from their darkest moments, shining brighter than ever before.

Tammy is uniquely qualified to guide readers through the storm because she has faced it head-on herself. Living with Sjögren's Disease and Alopecia while single-handedly raising two daughters without stable father figures has given her a wealth of experience and wisdom. As a business owner of Time 2 S.H.I.N.E. Consulting Services, LLC, and a Maxwell Leadership Certified Trainer, Speaker, and Coach, she empowers others to harness their inner strength. With over 23 years in the Air Force, where she not only thrived as a Logistics leader but also taught Leadership and Strategy at the graduate level, was a certified Resilience Trainer, and a Suicide Prevention/Violence Awareness Facilitator. Tammy knows how to navigate the complexities of leadership and resilience. Additionally, as a board member of the Sjögren's Foundation, she brings a passionate commitment to spreading awareness and support for those affected by chronic illness.

Now is the time to take action. Dive into ***SHINE Through the Storm*** and discover how to transform your struggles into stepping stones toward success. Let Tammy Dotson's story ignite your passion and empower you to reclaim your strength and purpose. Your journey begins now—embrace the empowerment that awaits!

UNLEASH YOUR INNER STRENGTH: YOU CAN'T STOP ME!

Feeling lost or overwhelmed in your life's journey? You're not alone—and you don't have to navigate your personal storms without support.

Introducing the Empowerment Package: You Can't Stop Me!

Discover the *key to resilience* by mastering your unique personality style, strengths, communication approach, and motivators. This transformative package empowers you to:

- **Navigate obstacles** with confidence and clarity

- **Show up authentically** in relationships and personal pursuits

- **Harness your unique skills** to thrive, not just survive

Imagine facing challenges with unwavering confidence—overcoming barriers to unleash the powerful woman within you. **You are capable, strong, and unstoppable!**

Are you ready to take the first step towards empowerment? Don't wait!

🗓 **Sign up today for a complimentary 15-minute DISCovery session at [https://coaching.time2shineconsulting.com](http://coaching.time2shineconsulting.com)** and start your journey toward resilience and unforgettable personal growth.

Your storm is temporary. Shine bright and let your true self emerge!

Made in the USA
Columbia, SC
21 June 2025

59306370R00070